Old English Literature
A Practical Introduction

Randolph Quirk
Valerie Adams
Derek Davy

Edward Arnold

First published 1975 by
Edward Arnold (Publishers) Ltd
25 Hill Street, London W1X 8LL

Cloth ISBN: 0 7131 5807 7
Paper ISBN: 0 7131 5808 5

Printed in Great Britain by Billing & Sons Limited, Guildford and London

Contents

Acknowledgments

We are grateful to the Dean and Chapter of Exeter Cathedral for permitting us to use the manuscript illustration on the cover and jacket (cf. 2.3); to numerous colleagues, but especially Marie Collins, John Dodgson, Peter Goolden, Geoffrey Needham, Noel Burton-Roberts and Catherine Sweetman, for help generously given at various stages; and to our students at University College London, who energetically responded over the years to trial versions of the material – *georne leorningcnihtas hira lārēowas lǣrende.*

1 Introduction

1.1 *The Beginnings of 'Englaland'*

For almost four hundred years from about AD 50, 'Britannia' was a province of the Roman Empire. With the recall of the legions in the early fifth century to help in the hopeless task of preventing imperial collapse, opportunity presented itself to the westward-pressing Germanic peoples to cross the North Sea. It was they who, overcoming the Celtic inhabitants, set in train the events through which the country came to be called 'Englaland', the land of the Angles.

We know little of the first 150 years of the Anglo-Saxon settlement, since the new masters – for all their vigour and stern virtues – were a basically illiterate society, with no conception of recording their activities in writing. But from about AD 600, successful missions began to bring Christianity to the English in a two-pronged movement: an advance of Celtic Christianity into Northumbria from Ireland and Scotland, and from Rome itself a mission to Kent (597) led by Augustine. Not only the Scriptures but a wide variety of learning began to be painstakingly set down on vellum in the English monastic houses that sprang up and which (under the leadership of such scholars as Alcuin, Aldhelm and Bede) soon made England a far-famed European centre for learning.

1.2 The Anglo-Saxons (as modern scholars usually call the English of the period before the Norman Conquest) were the first of the Germanic peoples – the first by some centuries – to achieve the literacy which enabled them to bring classical learning to bear upon ideals of heroism already highly developed in their continental forbears, as we know from Tacitus (see p. 20). And they did this while an apparently vigorous oral tradition still preserved the songs, tales, and myths of that earlier, pagan 'Germania'. It was by means of this literacy and this laborious handiwork on vellum that the Anglo-Saxons were able to give us a literature which reflects alike their Germanic interests and ideals, a deep Christian piety, and some considerable influence of Mediterranean learning. It was on vellum too that they came to develop their extraordinary skill in design and illumination (as in the Lindisfarne Gospels), matching the delicate and intricate jewellery in gold and silver (as in the Sutton Hoo treasure, which demonstrates most signally perhaps the high civilization that was achieved early in Anglo-Saxon England).

1.3 But it must be remembered that, in the first instance and always for the most part, the language of literacy was Latin. It was Latin (to a lesser extent Greek) that scholars read and it was in Latin that they wrote – a situation that persisted throughout the Middle Ages, only gradually changing thereafter. It was in Latin, after all, that Francis Bacon chose to perpetuate his major work – when Shakespeare was already dead.

Yet despite the serious religious, moral, and educational purposes which naturally had first call on the skill of scribes and the enormously expensive vellum writing material, the cultivated Anglo-Saxons in the early generations of their literacy and conversion to Christianity showed sufficient interest in their traditional poetry to commit a good deal of it to writing. Fortunately for us. As a result, here again England had a comfortable headstart on any of the post-imperial 'emerging peoples' of Europe in evolving – perhaps under the influence of the Irish – a vernacular literature: writing down works of imagination in their mother-tongue.

1.4 *Poetic Form*

It is not certain how much of the OE literature that we know had been handed down orally from generation to generation before being put into writing. But the *form* of the poetry was certainly traditional, as we can tell by comparing it with the closely similar verse (much smaller in extent and written down only much later) in the continental Old Saxon, Old High German, and Old Scandinavian. And it was a kind of poetry that lent itself readily to memorization and hence to oral transmission.

Basically, the form is a couplet structure, where each unit has two heavily stressed syllables, with a fairly free number of unstressed syllables, and where the two units are linked not by syllabic 'end-rhymes' (as in later rhyming poetry) but by 'head-rhymes' of syllable-initial sounds, i.e. alliteration. Imitated in Modern English, we might have:

> **Al**óne by the **l**áke   for**l**órnly he stánds,
> **w**áits **w**ónderingly.   A **w**índ stirs his háir,
> **b**réathes on his cúrls,   and re**b**úkes sádness.

As in the example, editions of OE poetry present the couplets horizontally, with a space between the two units or 'half-lines' as they are often called. The example further shows that it is only stressed syllables that alliterate, and that either one or two of these may alliterate in the first unit, but only the first of them in the second unit. But we have attempted to illustrate two other features of the poetry: the fact that major syntactic breaks frequently come between the alliteratively-linked units, and that a second half-line is frequently linked by a sort of paraphrase relation called 'variation' with the following first half-line (with which there is of course no alliterative or other metrical link). It will be seen that alliteration and variation subserve the purpose of memorization. The latter device also contributes much to the stately (at times somewhat ponderous) rhetoric and leisured pace of the poetry.

Some further striking characteristics have not been illustrated. Anglo-Saxon poets had at their disposal a large poetic vocabulary (items that are largely absent, that is, from OE prose); for example *mēce* 'sword', which, with *brand*, the ordinary word *sweord*, and other synonyms, provided a valuable resource when a particular alliterative sequence was needed. Secondly, poets often used words metaphorically: *brand* literally means something burning. Frequently these metaphors (or 'kennings' as they are called) are compounds such as *life-house* 'body', or phrases such as *whale's way* 'sea'. Thirdly, a considerable part of the poet's repertoire consisted of frameworks or 'formulae' for metrical units which could be used, with appropriate alteration, in different contexts: compare 4.1.26 and 4.1.293.

1.5 *Poetic Content*

It would be rash to judge the concerns of Anglo-Saxon poets purely on the actually surviving OE poetry. It is impossible to know how much was ever written down, or the proportion of what was written down that has survived. We know that there were devastating losses of manuscripts in the early destructive raids by the Vikings on Lindisfarne (793) and other such centres; so much so that King Alfred could complain (c. 890) that learning – indeed literacy itself – was on the verge of extinction. We know too that it is to the resurgence of learning during the Benedictine Revival (c. 950–1000, associated with Æthelwold, Dunstan, and Ælfric, for example) that we owe the manuscripts containing almost all the OE literature that has come down to us. And we may safely infer that, with the urgency of this work (struggling on into the troubled time of Æthelred when the country was torn by internal strife and by far more determined attacks from Scandinavia), the recording of purely secular poetry would have small claim on men's time and materials.

When we consider in addition the dangers of loss through fire, or lack of interest, or the dissolution of the monasteries, it would be foolish to think that the poetry that we still have (almost all of it in four manuscript volumes dating from c. 1000) was all the poetry set down in this period. One of these four codices chanced to be found in Vercelli, in northern Italy, where it had doubtless lain for hundreds of years unread because incomprehensible; yet in this is preserved, for example, the magnificent *Dream of the Rood*. And while three of the volumes are rather single-mindedly concerned with work of an explicitly religious or didactic nature, one – the Exeter Book – contains such a wealth and variety of work whose existence could not otherwise have been suspected, that it is not difficult to envisage the loss of other poems similarly imbued with a unique sensibility.

1.6 So one must speak only of the content and recurrent themes of that portion of OE poetry which has fortunately survived. Certain important characteristics leap out. Whether poets are treating classical myth (as in the *Phoenix*), testing their ingenuity with Riddles, setting Biblical themes to verse as in *Genesis*, or even attempting to recapture the horror and the glory of the Crucifixion, their imagination was fired by the heroic ideals of secular society and their language permeated with the concept of the lonely struggle against overwhelming forces. In this spirit too they looked in gloomy wonder on the massive Roman remains, ramparts and the ruins of once noble villas which they knew were beyond their ability to reproduce, and reflected on the mutability of worldly possessions and the inexorability of a fate that could overwhelm even men capable of such work (cf. 4.7.75ff.).

In short, the Anglo-Saxon poet was equipped, by his own interests and by the slow dignity of his poetic form, to deal above all in tragedy: man's predicament in the face of hostility, with only his ideals (especially loyalty to his lord – on earth or in heaven) securely beyond the reach of evil: cf. 4.1.230–37; 4.5.42–5.

1.7 *Prose Literature*

So far, we have spoken only of poetry: appropriately enough in a book where an introduction to OE poetry is the chief concern; appropriately, too, since in Anglo-Saxon England (as appears to be normal in a society), the development of a literary prose came later than that of the poetry. Nonetheless, it must be stated plainly that the prose achievement in Old English (again, especially with reference to the other vernaculars of Europe) is if anything even more striking than the poetic achievement. Here, after all, the Anglo-Saxons were, so far as we know, starting from scratch, with no native models (e.g. a prose story tradition) to draw on. But already in the ninth century King Alfred is calling for books in English prose (needed because the teaching of Latin had so sharply declined), and is indeed taking part himself in the task with the translation, for example, of St Gregory's *Cura Pastoralis*. By Ælfric's time, a century later, an excellent prose tradition had developed (of which he was one of the best exponents); we had homilies; history; translations from both the Old and New Testaments; laws and charters; works on medicine, science, philosophy; and even some fiction.

1.8 *This Book*

It is with a selection of such prose that we begin textual work in this book, since it is easy to find passages of prose elementary enough to begin a reading of OE. As well as serving to give the student a glimpse of the wide range of prose, the short extracts 3.1–4 will be the initial material for learning the basic vocabulary and grammar of the language.

The reader should therefore study each of the passages in turn with great care, following the explanatory glosses on the facing pages (non-literal translations are given in quotation marks) and referring constantly to the Outlines of the Language (5.1ff.). He will find that, although a given word is always translated for him more than once, he is expected to begin remembering the meanings of words, and the relations indicated by case endings and other inflected forms, without necessarily receiving further help. He can always, however, turn to the glossary at the end of the book in case of need.

1.9 To make it easier to relate the OE text to the translations and glosses on the facing pages, the prose passages are set out in lines which, where possible, do not break up grammatical units.

1.10 The first of the prose passages is from the annual Chronicle of events (also initiated in Alfred's time) which is a major source of our knowledge of Anglo-Saxon history. Passage 3.1 begins with the record of Byrhtnoth's defeat at Maldon, an event which is the subject of the heroic poem printed here almost in entirety as 4.1. This text too the student is advised to read strictly in turn. Along with 3.1–4, it constitutes a graded sequence where the glossing and annotation are designed to effect a progressive learning of the language. And it will be noticed that, in order to help the student still more to learn OE basically through these texts, we have deliberately drawn from them most of the examples used to illustrate the points of grammar set out in 5.1ff. Once he has mastered these initial texts, however, he should be in a position to move out of sequence in 4.2–8 if he so wishes.

1.11 *Additional Reading*

It is impossible in so small a book to present the reader with all the information on history and culture or all the critical discussion of the literature that he will find necessary. The following books are recommended for supplementary reading:

D. Whitelock, *The Beginnings of English Society* (rev. edn, Harmondsworth 1968)
D. M. Wilson, *The Anglo-Saxons* (rev. edn, Harmondsworth 1971)
T. A. Shippey, *Old English Verse* (London 1972)
S. B. Greenfield, *A Critical History of Old English Literature* (New York 1965)

2 The Sound of Old English

2.1 It is vital – especially if we are to appreciate the poetry – to acquire the habit of pronouncing OE as it sounded in the last century or so before the Norman Conquest. Although many letters (especially consonants) had the same values as in Modern English, there were numerous sharp differences, and in general the 'continental' values of letters (especially German values) are a better guide than those of ModE. In particular, it needs practice to remember that there were no 'silent letters' in OE: we must pronounce the initial letters of *wrītan* 'write', *cniht* 'boy', *gnornian* 'mourn', *hring* 'ring', the *r*'s and *e*'s in words like *hyrde* 'shepherd', and the lengthened (double) consonants in words like *hātte* 'was called'.

2.2 In the following key, the symbols in [ ] are those of the International Phonetic Association, and it is these that are used in the specimen transcription (2.3). In the right-hand column, alternative guidance is given by reference to ModE or (where specified) to particular varieties of English or to other modern languages.

Letter	*Example and its meaning*	*Conditions upon a specific value*	*IPA symbol*	*Modern example*
æ	sæt 'sat'		[æ]	*S.Brit.Eng.* sat
ǣ	dǣd 'deed'		[ɛ:]	*French* bête
a	mann 'man'	*before* m, n(g)	[ɒ]	*Amer.Eng.* hot
	dagas 'days'		[ɑ]	*German* Land
ā	hām 'home'		[ɑ:]	father
c	cyrice 'church'	*before/after* i, *often* æ, e, y	[tʃ]	*ch*urch
	cēne 'bold'		[k]	*k*een
cg	ecg 'edge'		[dʒ]	e*dge*
e	settan 'set'		[ɛ]	s*e*t
ē	hē 'he'		[e:]	*German* Leben
ea	earm 'arm'		[æə]	*as for* [æ], [ɛ:], [e], [e:], *followed by the first syllable of* about
ēa	ēare 'ear'		[ɛ:ə]	
eo	eorl 'nobleman'		[eə]	
ēo	bēor 'beer'		[e:ə]	
f	ǣfre 'ever'	*between voiced sounds*	[v]	e*v*er
	fīf 'five'		[f]	*f*i*f*e
g	gȳt 'yet'	*before/after* i, *usu. also* æ, e, y	[j]	*y*et
	fugol 'bird'	*between back vowels*	[ɣ]	*colloq. German* sagen
	gān 'go'		[g]	*g*o
h	heofon 'heaven'	*initially*	[h]	*h*eaven
	niht 'night'	*after* æ, e, i, y	[ç]	*German* i*ch*
	brōhte 'brought'	*after* a, o, u	[x]	*German* bra*ch*te
i	sittan 'sit'		[i]	s*i*t
ī	wīd 'wide'		[i:]	w*ee*d
o	monn 'man'	*before* m, n(g)	[ɒ]	*Amer.Eng.* hot
	God 'God'		[ɔ]	*Brit.Eng.* hot

Letter	*Example and its meaning*	*Conditions upon a specific value*	*IPA symbol*	*Modern example*
ō	gōd 'good'		[o:]	*German* Sohn
s	rīsan 'rise'	*between vowels*	[z]	ri*s*e
	hūs 'house'		[s]	hou*s*e
sc	scip 'ship'		[ʃ]	*sh*ip
þ, ð	ōþer, ōðer 'other'	*between vowels*	[ð]	o*th*er
	þurh, ðurh 'through'		[θ]	*th*rough
u	ful 'full'		[u]	f*u*ll
ū	hūs 'house'		[u:]	g*oo*se
y	wynn 'joy'		[y]	*German* würde
ȳ	rȳman 'make way'		[y:]	*German* Güte

2.3 The following short poem (see 4.8) is interlined with a phonetic transcription for practice reading. In this book, as is usual in modern editions of OE work, most of the letters and letter shapes of the original manuscripts are replaced by forms familiar in ModE. The exceptions are *æ*, *ð*, and *þ* (which imitate the manuscript forms) and the 'length marks' on vowels (which – like punctuation and capitalization – are editorial). The Anglo-Saxon mode of writing can be seen by comparing what follows with the reproduction on the cover and jacket, which has been adapted from the manuscript.

Wiht cwōm gongan þǣr weras sǣton
[wiçt kwo:m gɒŋgan θɛ:r wɛras sɛ:tɔn]
monige on mæðle, mōde snottre;
[mɒnijə ɔn mæðlə mo:də snɔtrə]
hæfde ān ēage ond ēaran twā,
[hævdə ɑ:n ɛ:əjə ɒnd ɛ:ərɑn twɑ:]
ond twēgen fēt, twelf hund hēafda,
[ɒnd twe:jən fe:t twɛlf hund hɛ:əvda]
hrycg ond wombe ond honda twā,
[hrydʒ ɒnd wɒmbə ɒnd hɒnda twɑ:]
earmas ond eaxle, ānne swēoran
[æərmas ɒnd æəkslə ɑ:n:ə swe:ərɑn]
ond sīdan twā. Saga hwæt ic hātte.
[ɒnd si:dɑn twɑ: saɣa hwæt itʃ hɑ:t:ə]

2.4 Spelling was not fixed, as it is in ModE under the rigorous constraints of the printed word. For example, the letters *þ* and *ð* were used almost interchangeably; words normally having a double consonant are sometimes found with a single consonant (*hysas* 4.1.107 beside *hyssas* 4.1.96); *ǣ* is sometimes replaced by *ā* (*þām* 3.1.3, *þār* 3.2.12); there is vacillation between *eal(l)* and *al* 'all', *and* and *ond*, *sweord* and *swurd* 'sword'. In 3.2 we find the spellings *cyning*, *cyningc*, and *cyngc* for 'king'. But above all, there was variation with *i*, *y*, and *ie*: *hit* and *hyt* (cf. 3.4.2); *hī* and *hȳ* 'they'; *gif*, *gyf* 'if'; *micel*, *mycel* 'great' (cf. 3.1.5); *clipian*, *clypian* 'call' (cf. 4.1.9); *sȳ* and *sīe* 'be' (cf. 3.4.10); *gyldan*, *gieldan* 'pay' (cf. 3.4.8). See also 5.11.

3 Prose

3.1 England under Attack

991. Hēr wæs Gypeswīc gehergod; ond æfter þām
swīðe raðe wæs Brihtnōð ealdorman[1] ofslægen
æt Mældūne.[2] Ond on þām gēare man gerǣdde
þæt man geald ǣrest[3] gafol Deniscan mannum[4]
for þām mycclan brōgan þe hī worhtan be þām sǣriman; 5
þæt wæs ǣrest tȳn þūsend punda.
Þæne rǣd gerǣdde Siric arcebiscop.
992. Hēr Ōswald, se ēadiga arcebiscop, forlēt þis līf
ond gefērde þæt heofonlīce; ond Æðelwine ealdorman
gefōr on þām ilcan gēare. Đā gerǣdde se cyng[5] 10
ond ealle his witan þæt man gegaderode þā scipu
þe āhtes wǣron tō Lundenbyrig. Ond se cyng
þā betǣhte þā fyrde tō lǣdenne Ælfrīce ealdorman
ond Þorode eorl[6] ond Ælfstāne biscop ond Æscwīge biscop;
ond sceoldan cunnian gif hī meahton þone here āhwǣr 15
ūtene betræppan. Đā sende se ealdorman Ælfrīc
ond hēt warnian þone here; ond þā on þǣre nihte,
ðe hī on ðone dæg tōgædere cuman sceoldon,
ðā sceōc hē on niht fram þǣre fyrde
him sylfum tō mycclum bismore; ond se here þā ætbærst, 20
būton ān scip þǣr man ofslōh. Ond þā gemētte se here
ðā scipu of Ēastenglum[7] ond of Lundene; ond hī ðǣr
ofslōgon mycel wæl, ond þæt scip genāmon
eall gewǣpnod ond gewǣdod þe se ealdorman on wæs.

These annals are from the Laud MS oft he Anglo-Saxon Chronicle, cf. 1. 10.

[1] *Brihtnoð ealdorman* An ealdorman was an official deputy appointed by the king to govern a part of the country. Ealdorman Brihtnoð (or Byrhtnoð, as the name is spelt in 4.1) governed Essex, the territory of the East Saxons, which included the modern county of Essex.

[2] *Mældūne* Maldon, in Essex.

[3] In fact tribute had been paid to the Vikings in King Alfred's time, over a hundred years earlier. But following the battle mentioned here, the ealdormen of Kent, Hampshire, and Wessex were forced to buy peace from the Scandinavians in this way.

[4] The Viking raiders are here referred to as 'Danes'; in Æthelred's time they included men from Norway as well as Denmark.

1 *Hēr* Here, 'At this point (in the Annals)'; *wæs* was (5.21); *Gypeswīc* Ipswich; *gehergod* plundered; *ond* and; *æfter þām* after that (5.10)
2 *swīðe* very; *raðe* soon; *ofslægen* slain
3 *on þām gēare* in that year (5.5); *man gerǣdde* one decided (5.17), 'it was decided' (5.26)
4 *þæt* that; *geald* paid (5.18); *ǣrest* first; *gafol* tribute; *þæt . . . gafol* 'that tribute should be paid for the first time'; *Deniscan mannum* to the Danish men
5 *for* on account of; *þām mycclan brōgan* the great terror (5.6); *þe* which, that (5.10); *hī* they (5.9); *worhtan* = *worhton* (5.11) wrought, had brought about (5.25); *be þām sǣriman* along the sea-coast
6 *tȳn þūsend punda* ten thousand pounds
7 *Þæne* = *Þone* (5.11) The, That; *rǣd* plan; *Þæne...* Archbishop Siric decided on that plan
8 *se ēadiga* the blessed (5.5); *forlēt* gave up; *þis līf* this life
9 *geferde* reached; *þæt heofonlīce* the heavenly [life]
10 *gefōr* departed [this life]; *on þām ilcan gēare* in the same year; *Ðā* Then; *se cyng* the king
11 *ealle* all; *witan* councillors; *man gegaderode* one assembled (cf. 3); *þā scipu* the ships (5.5)
12 *āhtes* of any account (5.13); *wǣron* were; *tō Lundenbyrig* at London; *Ðā . . . Lundenbyrig* Then the king and all his councillors decided that the ships that were worth anything should be assembled at London
13 *þā* then; *betǣhte* appointed; *þā fyrde* the [English] army; *tō lǣdenne* to lead; *Ond . . . biscop* And the king then appointed ealdorman Ælfric . . . and Bishop Æscwig to lead the [English] army
15 *sceoldan* = *sceoldon* (5.11,20) [they] should, had to; *cunnian* try; *gif* if, whether; *hī* they; *meahton* might (5.20); *þone here* the [enemy] army; *āhwǣr* anywhere; *gif. . .* whether they could surround the enemy anywhere from outside
16 *ūtene* from outside; *betræppan* entrap; *sende* sent
17 *hēt* ordered; *warnian* to warn (5.26); *Ðā . . . here* Then the ealdorman Ælfric sent [a message] and ordered the enemy to be warned; *on þǣre nihte* in the night
18 *on ðone dæg* on the day; *tōgædere cuman* come together; *ond . . . sceoldon* 'and then during the night preceding the day on which they were to join battle'
19 *sceōc* hastened away; *fram þǣre fyrde* from the [English] army (5.5)
20 *him. . .* 'to his own great disgrace' (*mycclum bismore*) (5.14); *ætbærst* burst out, escaped
21 *būton* except; *ān* one; *þǣr* there; *man ofslōh* one destroyed (cf. 3); *būton. . .* 'except that one ship was destroyed there'; *gemētte* met
22 *of* from; *Ēastenglum* the East Anglians; *Lundene* London
23 *ofslōgon* slew; *mycel wæl* great slaughter; *ond . . . wæl* 'and they caused great slaughter there'; *genāmon* they captured
24 *gewǣpnod* weaponed; *gewǣdod* equipped; *ond . . .* and they captured the ship completely armed and equipped which the ealdorman was on

---

[5] i.e. Æthelred II, reigned 978–1016. He was called Æthelred *Unrǣd*, 'bad counsel' or 'folly' (cf. *rǣd*, 7 above), but he has come to be called 'the Unready'.

[6] An *eorl* was a man of the upper class; in the eleventh century, and earlier in parts of England dominated by the Danes, this term came to replace *ealdorman*.

[7] East Anglia included Norfolk and Suffolk, as it does today.

3.2 Apollonius and Arcestrates

Ðā ðā Arcestrates se cyningc hæfde þæt gewrit oferrǣd,
þā niste hē hwilcne forlidenne his dohtor nemde;
beseah ðā tō ðām þrim cnihtum ond cwæð: 'Hwilc ę̄ower is forliden?'
Ðā cwæð heora ān sē hātte Ardalius: 'Ic eom forliden.'
Se ōðer him andwirde ond cwæð: 'Swīga ðū. Ādl þē fornime, 5
þæt þū ne bēo hāl ne gesund. Mid mē þū bōccræft leornodest,
ond ðū nǣfre būton þāre ceastre geate fram mē ne cōme.
Hwār gefōre ðū forlidennesse?' Mid ðī þe se cyngc
ne mihte findan hwilc heora forliden wǣre,
hē beseah tō Apollonio ond cwæð: 'Nim ðū, Apolloni, 10
þis gewrit ond rǣd hit. Ēaðe mæg gewurðan
þæt þū wite þæt ic nāt, ðū ðe þār andweard wǣre.'
Ðā nam Apollonius þæt gewrit ond rǣdde. Ond, sōna swā
hē ongeat þæt hē gelufod wæs fram ðām mǣdene,
his andwlita eal ārēodode. Ðā se cyngc þæt geseah, 15
þā nam hē Apollonies hand, ond hine hwōn fram þām cnihtum
gewænde,
ond cwæð: 'Wāst þū þone forlidenan man?' Apollonius cwæð:
'Ðū gōda cyning, gif þīn willa bið, ic hine wāt.'
Ðā geseah se cyngc þæt Apollonius mid rōsan rude
wæs eal oferbrǣded. Þā ongeat hē þone cwyde, ond þus cwæð tō
him: 20
'Blissa, blissa, Apolloni, for ðām þe mīn dohtor gewilnað þæs,
ðe mīn willa is.'

This extract is taken (slightly adapted) from the Old English version of a popular medieval romance, *Apollonius of Tyre*. Apollonius is shipwrecked on the shores of Cyrene, where the daughter of King Arcestrates falls in love with him. She persuades her father to make Apollonius her tutor. When some young

1 *Ðā ðā* Then when (5.28); *cyn(in)g(c)* king; *hæfde oferrǣd* had read through; *þæt gewrit* the letter (5.5)
2 *niste* did not know (5.20,30); *hwilcne* which; *forlidenne* shipwrecked [man]; *dohtor* daughter; *nemde* had named (5.25)
3 *beseah tō* looked at; *ðām þrim cnihtum* the three young men; *cwæð* said; *Hwilc ēower* Which of you (5.9,13)
4 *heora* of them; *ān* one; *sē hātte* who was called (5.26); *Ic eom* I am
5 *Se ōðer* [One of] the other[s]; *andwirde* answered; *Swīga ðū* You be silent! (5.17); *Ādl* . . . 'May disease carry you off' (*fornime*, 5.18,27)
6 *þæt* so that; *ne bēo* may not be (5.21,29); *hāl ne gesund* healthy nor sound; *mid* with; *leornodest* learned; *bōccræft* book-learning
7 *nǣfre* never; *būton* outside; *þāre ceastre geate* the gate of the (*þāre*) town; *fram* away from; *cōme* came
8 *Hwār* = *Hwǣr* . . . 'Where did you experience shipwreck?' (*forlidennesse*); *Mid ðī þe* When
9 *mihte* could; *findan* find
10 *Nim* Take
11 *rǣd* read; *hit* it; *Ēaðe* . . . 'It may easily happen' (*gewurðan*)
12 *wite* may know (5.20,27); *þæt ic nāt* 'that [which] I do not know' (5.30); *þār* = *þǣr*; *andweard* present
13 *nam* took; *rǣdde* read; *sōna swā* as soon as
14 *ongeat* realized; *gelufod wæs* was loved (5.26); *fram* by; *mǣdene* maiden
15 *andwlita* face; *eal ārēodode* reddened all [over]; *geseah* saw (5.18)
16 *hwōn* a little way; *hine gewænde* went (5.23)
17 *wāst þū* do you know
18 *gōda* good (5.3); *gif* . . . *bið* if it is your will; *hine* him; *wāt* know
19 *mid rude* with the redness; *rōsan* of a rose
20 *oferbrǣded* overspread; *ongeat* understood; *þone cwyde* the speech, i.e. what Apollonius has just said; *þus* thus
21 *blissa* rejoice; *for ðām þe* because; *mīn* my; *gewilnað* desires; *þæs* that [thing] (5.23)

---

men seek her hand in marriage, Arcestrates asks her to choose which she will have. She writes a note, saying that she wishes to marry the man who has been shipwrecked.

3.3 A Preface by Ælfric

Ic Ælfrīc, munuc ond mæssepreost, swā þēah wāccre
þonne swilcum hādum gebyrige, wearð āsend on Æþelrēdes dæge
cyninges fram Ælfēage biscope, Aðelwoldes æftergengan,
tō sumum mynstre, þe is Cernel gehāten, þurh Æðelmǣres bēne
ðæs þegenes; his gebyrd ond goodnys sind gehwǣr cūþe. 5
Þā bearn mē on mōde (ic trūwige þurh Godes gife) þæt
ic ðās bōc of Ledenum gereorde tō Engliscre sprǣce āwende,
nā þurh gebylde micelre lāre, ac forþan þe ic geseah ond gehȳrde
mycel gedwyld on manegum Engliscum bōcum, þe ungelǣrede menn
þurh heora bilewitnysse tō micclum wīsdōme tealdon. Ond 10
mē ofhrēow þæt hī nē cūþon nē næfdon þā godspellīcan lāre
on heora gewritum, būton þām mannum ānum ðe þæt Leden cūðon,
ond būton þām bōcum ðe Ælfrēd cyning snoterlīce āwende of Ledene
on Englisc,[1] þā synd tō hæbbenne. For þisum antimbre
ic gedyrstlǣhte, on Gode trūwiende, þæt ic ðās gesetnysse undergann, 15
ond ēac for ðām þe menn behōfiað gōdre lāre swīðost on þisum
tīman,
þe is geendung þyssere worulde,[2] ond bēoð fela frēcednyssa
on mancynne ǣr ðan þe se ende becume, swā swā ūre Drihten
on his godspelle cwæð tō his leorningcnihtum, 'Đonne bēoð
swilce gedreccednyssa swilce nǣron nǣfre ǣr fram frymðe
middangeardes.'[3] 20

Ælfric (c.955 – c.1020) was trained at Winchester by Bishop Æthelwold, one of the leaders of the tenth-century revival of English monastic life and learning. He was sent in 987 to the newly established monastery of Cernel (Cerne Abbas, in Dorset) and there wrote, among many other works, the Catholic Homilies – two series of sermons designed to be delivered on holy days and saints' days throughout the Church year. This extract is part of his Preface to the first series. In 1005 Ælfric became abbot of another new monastery founded by Æthelmær, at Eynsham, near Oxford. His last work was probably written about 1010.

1 *munuc* monk; *mæssepreōst* mass-priest, 'priest competent to celebrate mass'; *swā þēah* although; *wāccre* weaker (5.8)
2 *þonne* than; *swilcum hādum* for such [holy] orders; *gebyrige* befits (5.27); *wearð āsend* was sent (5.26); *dæge* day
3 *cyninges* of the king; *æftergengan* successor
4 *tō sumum mynstre* to a certain monastery; *þe . . . gehāten* which is called Cernel; *þurh* through, because of; *bēne* request; *Æðelmǣres ðæs þegenes* of the thane Æðelmær
5 *gebyrd* birth, rank; *goodnys* goodness; *sind* are; *gehwǣr* everywhere; *cūþe* known
6 *bearn* [it] ran; *mōde* mind; *Þā . . . mōde* 'Then it occurred to me'; *trūwige* trust; *gife* gift, grace
7 *ðās bōc* this book (5.6f.); *of Ledenum gereorde* from the Latin language; *sprǣce* speech; *āwende* should translate
8 *nā* not at all; *gebylde* confidence; *micelre lāre* of great learning; *ac* but; *forþan* because; *gehȳrde* heard
9 *gedwyld* error, heresy; *on manegum* in many; *ungelǣrede* unlearned
10 *heora bilewitnysse* their simplicity; *tō* as, for; *wīsdōme* wisdom; *tealdon* considered (as), took (for)
11 *mē ofhrēow* I regretted (5.22); *nē . . . nē* neither . . . nor; *cūþon* knew; *næfdon* had not (5.30); *godspellīcan lāre* evangelical doctrine
12 *gewritum* writings; *būton* except; *ānum* only
13 *snoterlīce* wisely; *of* from
14 *þā . . . hæbbenne* which are to be had (5.26); *antimbre* reason
15 *gedyrstlǣhte* presumed; *trūwiende* trusting; *þæt* so that; *ðās gesetnysse* this work; *undergann* undertook
16 *ēac* also; *behōfiað* have need; *swīðost* especially; *on þisum tīman* at this time
17 *geendung* ending; *þyssere worulde* of this world; *bēoð* are, 'there will be' (5.24); *fela frēcednyssa* many calamities (5.13)
18 *mancynne* mankind; *ǣr ðan* before; *ende* end; *becume* occurs (5.27); *swā swā* just as; *ūre Drihten* our Lord
19 *godspelle* gospel; *leorningcnihtum* disciples; *Ðonne bēoð* 'Then there will be' (5.24)
20 *swilce* such (5.28); *gedreccednyssa* tribulations; *swilce . . .* as there have never been before since the beginning (*frymðe*) of the world (*middangeardes*)

---

[1] King Alfred (849–99) translated a number of influential works into English, including Gregory's *Pastoral Care* and Boethius' *Consolation of Philosophy*. The OE version of Bede's *Ecclesiastical History of the English People* is associated with him, as is the Anglo-Saxon Chronicle.

[2] It was a common belief that the world would end in the year 1000.

[3] Ælfric may be referring to Matthew 24,21, where Christ says, 'For then there will be great tribulation, such as has not been seen from the beginning of the world' (R.V.). His words in Mark 13,19 are very similar. Both passages go on to refer to 'false Christs' and deceptions; cf. Ælfric's own fears of *gedwyld*, 9 above.

3.4 A Miscellany

(*a*) Ǣlc trēow þe ne byrð gōdne wæstm,
sȳ hyt forcorfen and on fȳr āworpen.
Witodlīce, be hyra wæstmum gē hī oncnāwað.
Ne gǣð ǣlc þǣra on heofena rīce þe cwyþ tō mē,
'Drihten! Drihten!' ac sē þe wyrcð mīnes fæder willan 5
þe on heofenum is, sē gǣð on heofena rīce.

(*b*) Ðonne mon bēam on wuda forbærne, ond weorðe yppe
on þone ðe hit dyde, gielde hē fulwīte:
geselle siextig scillinga[1] – for þām þe fȳr bið þēof.[2]

(*c*) Gif man calu sīe, Plinius se micla lǣce[3] segþ þisne lǣcedōm. 10
Genim dēade bēon; gebærne tō ahsan; and linsǣd ēac;
dō ele tō on þæt. Sēoþe swīþe lange ofer glēdum.
Āsēoh þonne and āwringe; and nime welies lēaf, gecnuwige,
gēote on þone ele. Wylle eft hwīle on glēdum.
Āsēoh; þonne smire mid æfter baþe. 15

(*d*) Sanctus Paulus wæs gesēonde on norðanweardne þisne
middangeard,[4]
þǣr ealle wætero niðer gewītað, and hē þǣr geseah
ofer ðǣm wætere sumne hārne stān. And wǣron
norð of ðǣm stāne āwexene swīðe hrīmige bearwas,
and ðǣr wǣron þȳstro genipo, and under þǣm stāne 20
wæs nicera eardung and wearga. And hē geseah
þæt on ðǣm clife hangodan, on ðǣm īsgean bearwum,
manige swearte sāula, be heora handum gebundne.
And þā fȳnd þǣr on nicra onlīcnesse heora grīpende wǣron,
swā swā grǣdig wulf. And þæt wæter wæs sweart 25
under þǣm clife neoðan.

This selection further exemplifies the range of material in OE prose: the Anglo-Saxon had access to parts of the Bible, to the law, to medicine, and of course to homiletic teaching in his own language. The extract (*a*) is from Matthew 7,19–21; (*b*) is from the laws of Ine, an early king of Wessex; (*c*) is from an important British Museum manuscript, Bald's Leechbook, fol. 57b; (*d*) is from St Paul's vision of hell in the 17th of the Blickling Homilies, with striking parallels to the description of the sinister mere where Grendel's mother lurked (4.5).

1 *Ǣlc* Each; *trēow* tree; *ne byrð* does not bear (5.18); *gōdne wæstm* good fruit
2 *sȳ hyt* let it be (5.21,27); *forcorfen* cut down; *on* into; *fȳr* fire; *āworpen* thrown
3 *Witodlīce* Truly; *be* by; *hyra* their; *wæstmum* fruits; *gē* you (pl.); *hī* them; *oncnāwað* will distinguish (5.24)
4 *Ne gǣð* will not go (5.24); *þǣra* of those; *heofena rīce* kingdom of the heavens; *cwyþ* says
5 *Drihten* Lord; *ac* but; *sē þe* he who; *wyrcð* carries out; *mīnes fæder willan* my father's wishes
6 *gǣð* will go (5.24)
7 *Ðonne* When, 'If'; *mon* anyone; *bēam* a tree; *on wuda* in a wood; *forbærne* burn down (5.27); *weorðe* it become (5.27); *yþþe* manifest
8 *on* against; *þone . . .* him who did it; *gielde hē* let him pay (5.18,27); *fulwīte* full penalty
9 *geselle* let him hand over; *siextig* sixty; *scillinga* shillings (5.13); *bið* is; *þēof* a thief
10 *gif* if; *man* anyone; *calu* bald; *sīe* should be (5.27); *lǣce* leech, 'doctor'; *segþ* says, 'prescribes' (5.17); *lǣcedōm* remedy
11 *Genim* Take; *dēade* dead; *bēon* bees; *gebærne* [one] should burn [them] (5.27); *ahsan* ashes; *linsǣd* linseed; *ēac* also
12 *dō tō* apply; *ele* oil; *on þæt* to it; *sēoþe* boil (5.27); *swīþe* very; *lange* long; *ofer* over; *glēdum* coals, 'open fire'
13 *Āsēoh* Strain; *þonne* then; *āwringe* squeeze (5.27); *nime* take (5.27); *welies* of willow; *lēaf* leaves; *gecnuwige* crush (5.27)
14 *gēote on þone ele* pour the oil on (5.27); *Wylle* Boil (5.27); *eft* again; *hwīle* for a while (5.12)
15 *smire mid* smear with [the substance]; *baþe* bath
16 *wæs gesēonde* gazed (5.24); *on* towards; *norðanweardne þisne middangeard* the northward [part of] this world
17 *þǣr* where; *ealle* all; *wætero* = *wæteru* (5.11) waters; *niðer* down; *gewītað* go; *þǣr* there
18 *ofer ðǣm wætere* above the water; *sumne* a certain; *hārne* grey; *stān* stone, rock; *wǣron āwexene* 'had sprung up'
19 *norð* north; *hrīmige* frost-covered; *bearwas* woods
20 *þȳstro* dark; *genipo* = *genipu* mists
21 *nicera* of water-monsters; *eardung* dwelling-place; *wearga* of evil creatures
22 *clife* cliff; *hangodan* = *hangodon* (5.11) hung; *īsgean* = *īsigum* (5.11) ice-covered
23 *swearte* black, 'sinful'; *sāula* souls; *be* by; *gebundne* bound
24 *þā fȳnd* the fiends; *onlīcnesse* likeness, form; *heora grīpende wǣron* were attacking them (5.23,24)
25 *swā swā* just as; *grǣdig wulf* a greedy wolf
26 *under neoðan* underneath

---

[1] The amount can be gauged from the fact that an ox was valued at about six shillings.

[2] Fire is thus equated with theft through its silent 'stealth'; the punishment for theft was also 60 shillings.

[3] Pliny the Elder (died AD 79), from whom much medieval medical and scientific lore was derived.

[4] The world was conceived as occupying a middle point, with the waters and the forces of evil around and beneath.

4 Poetry

4.1 The Battle of Maldon

Ðā þǣr Byrhtnōð ongan beornas trymian,
rād and rǣdde, rincum tǣhte
hū hī sceoldon standan, and þone stede healdan,
and bæd þæt hyra randas rihte hēoldon
fæste mid folman, and ne forhtedon nā.[1] 5
Þā hē hæfde þæt folc fægere getrymmed,
hē līhte þā mid lēodon, þǣr him lēofost wæs,
þǣr hē his heorðwerod holdost wiste.
Þā stōd on stæðe,[2] stīðlīce clypode
wīcinga ār, wordum mǣlde, 10
sē on bēot ābēad brimlīþendra
ǣrende tō þām eorle, þǣr hē on ōfre stōd:
'Mē sendon tō þē sǣmen snelle,
hēton ðē secgan, þæt þū mōst sendan raðe
bēagas[3] wið gebeorge; and ēow betere is 15
þæt gē þisne gārrǣs mid gafole forgyldon,
þonne wē swā hearde hilde dǣlon.
Ne þurfe wē ūs spillan, gif gē spēdaþ tō þām;
wē willað wið þām golde grið fæstnian.
Gyf þū þæt gerǣdest þe hēr rīcost eart, 20
þæt þū þīne lēoda lȳsan wille,
syllan sǣmannum on hyra sylfra dōm
feoh wið frēode, and niman frið æt ūs,
wē willaþ mid þām sceattum ūs tō scype gangan,
on flot fēran, and ēow friþes healdan.' 25
Byrhtnōð maþelode, bord hafenode,[4]
wand wācne æsc, wordum mǣlde,

This battle is mentioned briefly in the Anglo-Saxon Chronicle for the year 991 (see 3.1) as one of a series of disastrous encounters with the Vikings. In view of its historical background as we have it in the Chronicle, the poem is remarkable for the degree to which it is inspired by the heroic system of values of the pre-migration Germanic societies. This is described 900 years earlier by Tacitus: 'The chiefs fight for victory, the companions for their chief' (*Germania*, AD 97–8, ch. 14; here, and in subsequent notes, we have used the Penguin translation, 1970). We have omitted a few lines at the beginning and end of the poem, which in any case has not been preserved in its entirety.

[1] The soldiers to whom Byrhtnoð is giving these very explicit instructions are the local conscripts, belonging to the *fyrd*. They are distinct from Byrhtnoð's

1 *ongan* (5.24). . . proceeded to rally (*trymian*) the men (*beornas*)
2 *rād* rode; *rǣdde* instructed; *rincum* (5.23) . . . explained (*tǣhte*) to the warriors
3 *hū* how; *þone* . . . hold (*healdan*) the position (*stede*)
4 *bæd* commanded; *hyra randas* their shields; *rihte* correctly; *hēoldon* = *hēolden* (5.11) they should hold (5.27)
5 *mid folman* = *folmum* (5.11) with hands; *and* . . . and [that] they should never (*nā*) be afraid
6 *folc* company; *fægere* suitably; *getrymmed* rallied
7 *līhte* alighted; *mid lēodon* = *lēodum* (5.11) among the people; *þǣr*. . . where, to him, it was most pleasing (*lēofost*) [to be]
8 *þǣr* where (5.28); *his* . . . knew (*wiste*) his most devoted (*holdost*) hearth-troop [to be]
9 *stæðe* shore; *stīðlīce* sternly; *clypode* called out
10 *wīcinga* of the Vikings; *ār* messenger; *wordum* with words; *mǣlde* spoke
11 *sē* who; *on bēot* in challenge; *ābēad* proclaimed; *brimlīþendra* of the sea-travellers
12 *ǣrende* message; *ōfre* shore
13 *þē* you (sg.); *sǣmen* seamen; *snelle* bold
14 *hēton* . . . ordered [me] to say (*secgan*) to you; *raðe* quickly
15 *bēagas* rings; *wið gebeorge* in return for protection; *ēow* for you (pl.); *betere* better
16 *gārrǣs* spear-rush, i.e. battle (5.35); *mid* . . . should buy off (*forgyldon*, 5.11) with tribute (*gafole*)
17 *þonne* . . . than [that] we should join in (*dǣlon*, 5.11) such hard battle (*hilde*)
18 *Ne þurfe wē* We need not (5.20); *ūs* ourselves; *spillan* destroy; *gif* . . . if you are prosperous to that extent, i.e. 'if you can manage to pay'
19 *willað* are willing; *wið* in return for; *grið* truce; *fæstnian* to establish
20 *Gyf*. . . If you decide (*gerǣdest*) that; *þe* . . . who are the mightiest here
21 *þæt* with the following clause expands *þæt* in 20 (5.28); *þīne* . . . will ransom (*lȳsan*) your people (5.27)
22 *syllan* give; *sǣmannum* to the seamen; *on* . . . according to their own judgment (*dōm*)
23 *feoh* money; *wið frēode* in return for peace; *frið* peace; *æt* from
24 *mid þām sceattum* with the payments; *ūs gangan* 'betake ourselves'; *scype* ship
25 *flot* the sea; *fēran* go; *ēow* . . . keep peace with you
26 *maþelode* spoke; *bord* shield; *hafenode* raised
27 *wand* brandished; *wācne* slender; *æsc* ash-wood [spear]

---

own expert retainers, referred to in 8 as the 'hearth-troop'; cf. *heorðgenēatas*, 188.

[2] *on stæðe* The Vikings had sailed up the estuary of the river Blackwater (here called Panta, 52, 81) to the island of Northey, which is still linked to the mainland by a ford or causeway (*bricg*, 58), exposed only at low tide.

[3] *bēagas* The literal reference is to ornamental gold rings, or 'torcs', which were both a feature of Anglo-Saxon jewellery and a symbol of wealth. Had it been paid, the tribute referred to by the Viking messenger would probably have taken the form of a collection of arms, ornaments and other items of value.

[4] *bord hafenode* A gesture to receive attention; cf. 228 and 293; similarly, 214.

yrre and ānrǣd   āgeaf him andsware:
'Gehȳrst þū, sǣlida,   hwæt þis folc segeð?
Hī willað ēow tō gafole   gāras syllan,   30
ǣttrene ord   and ealde swurd,[5]
þā heregeatu[6] þe ēow   æt hilde ne dēah.
Brimmanna boda,   ābēod eft ongēan,
sege þīnum lēodum   miccle lāþre spell,
þæt hēr stynt unforcūð   eorl mid his werode,   35
þe wile gealgian   ēþel þysne,
Æþelrēdes eard,   ealdres mīnes
folc and foldan; feallan sceolon
hǣþene æt hilde.   Tō hēanlic mē þinceð
þæt gē mid ūrum sceattum   tō scype gangon   40
unbefohtene,   nū gē þus feor hider
on ūrne eard   in becōmon.
Ne sceole gē swā sōfte   sinc gegangan;
ūs sceal ord and ecg   ǣr gesēman,
grim gūðplega,   ǣr wē gofol syllon.'   45
   Hēt þā bord beran,   beornas gangan,
þæt hī on þām ēasteðe   ealle stōdon.
Ne mihte þǣr for wætere   werod tō þām ōðrum;
þǣr cōm flōwende   flōd æfter ebban,
lucon lagustrēamas.[7]   Tō lang hit him þūhte,   50
hwænne hī tōgædere   gāras bēron.
Hī þǣr Pantan strēam   mid prasse bestōdon
Ēastseaxena ord   and se æschere.
Ne mihte hyra ǣnig   ōðrum derian,
būton hwā þurh flānes flyht   fyl genāme.   55
Se flōd ūt gewāt;   þā flotan stōdon gearowe,
wīcinga fela,   wīges georne.
Hēt þā hæleða hlēo   healdan þā bricge
wigan wīgheardne,   sē wæs hāten Wulfstān,
cāfne mid his cynne   – þæt wæs Cēolan sunu –   60
þe ðone forman man   mid his francan ofscēat,
þe þǣr baldlīcost   on þā bricge stōp.
Þǣr stōdon mid Wulfstāne   wigan unforhte,
Ælfere and Maccus,   mōdige twēgen,
þā noldon æt þām forda   flēam gewyrcan,   65
ac hī fæstlīce   wið ðā fȳnd weredon,

---

[5] *ealde swurd* Weapons were valuable items of property and were handed down from father to son. Old swords were naturally the best, since they would have proved their worth.

[6] *heregeatu* 'A feudal service, originally consisting of weapons, horses, and other military equipments, restored to a lord on the death of his tenant' (OED s.v. *heriot*, 2). This was later converted to a money payment, which is what

28 *yrre* angry; *ānrǣd* resolute; *āgeaf* gave back; *andsware* answer
29 *Gehȳrst þū* Do you hear; *sǣlida* seafarer; *segeð* says
30 *Hī* They; *tō gafole* as tribute; *gāras* spears
31 *ǣttrene* deadly; *ord* point; *ealde* old; *swurd* (2.4) swords
32 *heregeatu* war-gear; *æt hilde* in battle; *dēah* profits (5.20,24)
33 *Brimmanna* of the seamen; *boda* messenger; *ābēod* . . . report back (*ongēan*) again (*eft*)
34 *þīnum lēodum* to your people; *miccle lāþre spell* a much uglier message
35 *stynt* stands; *unforcūð* noble; *werode* troop
36 *gealgian* defend; *ēþel þysne* this homeland
37 *eard* country; *ealdres mīnes* my lord's
38 *foldan* land; *feallan* . . . *hǣþene* the heathens shall fall
39 *hǣþene* heathens; *Tō hēanlic* Too shameful; *mē þinceð* it seems to me (5.22)
40 *gangon* = *gangen* should go (5.27)
41 *unbefohtene* unopposed; *nū* now that; *þus feor* thus far; *hider* hither
42 *becōmon* have come (5.25)
43 *swā sōfte* so easily; *sinc* treasure; *gegangan* gain
44 *ūs* . . . point and edge must first (*ǣr*) reconcile (*gesēman*) us
45 *gūðplega* war-play, i.e. battle; *gofol* tribute
46 *Hēt* He commanded; *bord beran* shields to be carried (5.26)
47 *þæt* so that; *ēasteðe* river-bank
48 *Ne* . . . There, because of the water, the army could not [get] to the others, i.e. the Vikings (5.20)
49 *flōwende* flowing; *flōd æfter ebban* the flood-tide after the ebb
50 *lucon lagustrēamas* the tidal currents interlocked; *hit* . . . it seemed to them
51 *hwænne* [until the time] when; *tōgædere* together; *bēron* = *bǣren* might bear
52 *mid prasse* with [military] pomp; *bestōdon* stood by
53 *ord* front line; *æschere* ash-wood [ship] ravagers (lit. sg.), i.e. the Vikings
54 *hyra ǣnig* any of them (5.13); *derian* harm (5.23)
55 *būton* except; *hwā* whoever; *þurh flānes flyht* because of an arrow's flight; *fyl* death; *genāme* received (5.27)
56 *ūt gewāt* went out; *þā flotan* the seamen; *gearowe* ready
57 *fela* many (5.13); *wīges* for battle; *georne* eager
58 *þā* then; *hæleða* of heroes; *hlēo* protector; *bricge* causeway
59 *wigan* warrior; *wīgheardne* battle-hard; *hāten* called
60 *cāfne* valiant; *mid his cynne* among his kinsmen; *Cēolan sunu* Ceola's son
61 *þe* . . . who with his spear (*francan*) shot down the first man
62 *baldlīcost* most boldly; *stōp* stepped
63 *wigan* warriors; *unforhte* unafraid
64 *mōdige twēgen* two brave [men]
65 *þā* who; *forda* ford; *flēam gewyrcan* take to flight
66 *ac* but, rather; *hī weredon* defended themselves; *fæstlīce* resolutely; *ðā fȳnd* the enemy (pl.)

---

the Vikings are demanding. They are indeed to receive the weapons of the English, but with an effect very different from that suggested by the later meaning of *heregeatu*.

[7] *lucon lagustrēamas* This may mean that the two tidal streams flowing round either side of the island joined here, or that the incoming tide met the current of the river.

þā hwīle þe hī wǣpna wealdan mōston.
Þā hī þæt ongēaton, and georne gesāwon
þæt hī þǣr bricgweardas bitere fundon,
ongunnon lytegian þā lāðe gystas: 70
bǣdon þæt hī upgangan āgan mōston,
ofer þone ford faran, fēþan lǣdan.
Ðā se eorl ongan for his ofermōde[8]
ālȳfan landes tō fela lāþere ðēode.
Ongan ceallian þā ofer cald wæter 75
Byrhtelmes bearn (beornas gehlyston):
'Nū ēow is gerȳmed, gāð ricene tō ūs,
guman tō gūþe; God āna wāt
hwā þǣre wælstōwe wealdan mōte.'
Wōdon þā wælwulfas, for wætere ne murnon, 80
wīcinga werod, west ofer Pantan,
ofer scīr wæter scyldas wēgon,
lidmen tō lande linde bǣron.
Þǣr ongēan gramum gearowe stōdon
Byrhtnōð mid beornum. Hē mid bordum hēt 85
wyrcan þone wīhagan,[9] and þæt werod healdan
fæste wið fēondum. Þā wæs feohte nēh,
tīr æt getohte; wæs sēo tīd cumen
þæt þǣr fǣge men feallan sceoldon.
Þǣr wearð hrēam āhafen, hremmas wundon, 90
earn ǣses georn;[10] wæs on eorþan cyrm.
Hī lēton þā of folman fēolhearde speru,
grimme gegrundene gāras flēogan;
bogan wǣron bysige, bord ord onfēng,
biter wæs se beadurǣs, beornas fēollon 95
on gehwæðere hand, hyssas lāgon.
Wund wearð Wulfmǣr, wælræste gecēas,
Byrhtnōðes mǣg, hē mid billum wearð,
his swustersunu,[11] swīðe forhēawen.
Þǣr wearð wīcingum wiþerlēan āgyfen: 100
gehȳrde ic þæt Ēadweard ānne slōge
swīðe mid his swurde, swenges ne wyrnde,
þæt him æt fōtum fēoll fǣge cempa;
þæs him his ðēoden þanc gesǣde,
þām būrþēne,[12] þā hē byre hæfde. 105

---

[8] *ofermōde* Cf. 4.2, where Satan comes to grief because of his *ofermētto* 'pride' (27). But the poet here clearly intends to praise Byrhtnoð's heroism, while at the same time pointing out the fatal miscalculation which resulted in defeat.

[9] *wīhagan* This defensive formation is called *scyldburh* in 226, *bordweall* in 261.

67 *þā hwīle þe* as long as; *wǣpna wealdan* wield weapons (5.23); *mōston* could
68 *ongēaton* perceived; *georne* clearly; *gesāwon* saw
69 *bricgweardas* bridge-guards; *bitere* fierce; *fundon* found
70 *ongunnon* began; *lytegian* to use guile; *lāðe* hateful; *gystas* foreigners
71 *bǣdon* they asked; *upgangan* passage up [on to land]; *āgan mōston* might have
72 *faran* to go; *fēþan lǣdan* to lead the troops
73 *ongan ālȳfan* allowed (5.24); *for his ofermōde* because of his great courage
74 *landes* land (5.13); *tō fela* too much; *lāþere ðēode* to the hateful people
75 *Ongan ceallian* called (5.24); *cald* cold
76 *Byrhtelmes bearn* Byrhtelm's son, i.e. Byrhtnoð; *gehlyston* paid attention
77 *ēow* . . . [the way] is opened for you; *gāð* advance; *ricene* quickly
78 *guman* men; *gūþe* battle; *āna* alone
79 *þǣre wælstōwe* the slaughter-place, i.e. battlefield (5.23); *wealdan mōte* may control
80 *Wōdon* advanced; *wælwulfas* slaughter-wolves (5.35); *for* . . . they did not care about the water
81 *wīcinga* see 10
82 *scīr* gleaming; *scyldas* shields; *wēgon* = *wǣgon* carried
83 *lidmen* sailors; *linde* lime-wood [shields]
84 *ongēan* against; *gramum* [the] fierce [ones]; *gearowe* ready
85 *mid bordum* with shields
86 *wyrcan* to be formed (5.26); *wīhagan* battle-hedge; *and* . . . and the company to hold firm against the enemy
87 *feohte* the fight; *nēh* = *nēah* near
88 *tīr* glory; *æt getohte* in battle; *wæs* . . . the time was come
89 *fǣge* doomed
90 *wearð* was; *hrēam* outcry; *āhafen* raised; *hremmas* ravens; *wundon* wheeled
91 *earn* the eagle; *ǣses* for carrion; *cyrm* uproar
92 *lēton flēogan* let fly; *fēolhearde* file-hard; *speru* spears
93 *grimme* cruelly; *gegrundene* sharpened
94 *bogan* bows; *bysige* busy; *bord* . . . the shield received the point
95 *beadurǣs* battle-rush
96 *gehwæðere* either; *hyssas* young men; *lāgon* lay dead
97 *Wund* wounded; *wælræste* bed of slaughter; *gecēas* chose
98 *mǣg* kinsman; *mid billum* with swords; *wearð forhēawen* was hewn down
99 *swustersunu* sister's son; *swīðe* cruelly
100 *wiþerlēan* recompense; *āgyfen* given
101 *gehȳrde ic* I heard; *þæt* . . . that Eadweard struck one
102 *swīðe* fiercely; *swenges* blow; *wyrnde* withheld (5.23)
103 *þæt* so that; *him* . . . at his feet (5.14); *cempa* warrior
104 *þæs* for that; *him* to him; *ðēoden* prince; *þanc* thanks; *gesǣde* said
105 *þām būrþēne* to the adjutant (see footnote 12); *byre* opportunity

---

[10] See 4.7.81–2 for another instance of this conventional theme of the 'beasts of battle'.

[11] *his swustersunu* Tacitus says, 'The sons of sisters are as highly honoured by their uncles as by their own fathers. Some tribes even consider the former tie the closer and more sacred of the two' (*Germania*, ch. 20).

[12] *būrþēne* A *būr* was a room or dwelling separate from the communal hall; *þēn, þegen* means 'servant' or 'follower'.

Swā stemnetton stīðhicgende
hysas æt hilde, hogodon georne
hwā þǣr mid orde ǣrost mihte
on fǣgean men feorh gewinnan,
wigan mid wǣpnum; wæl fēol on eorðan. 110
Stōdon stædefæste, stihte hī Byrhtnōð,
bæd þæt hyssa gehwylc hogode tō wīge,
þe on Denon wolde dōm gefeohtan.
Wōd þā wīges heard, wǣpen up āhōf,
bord tō gebeorge, and wið þæs beornes stōp. 115
Ēode swā ānrǣd eorl tō þām ceorle:[13]
ǣgþer hyra ōðrum yfeles hogode.
Sende ðā se sǣrinc sūþerne gār,
þæt gewundod wearð wigena hlāford;
hē scēaf þā mid ðām scylde, þæt se sceaft tōbærst, 120
and þæt spere sprengde, þæt hit sprang ongēan.
Gegremod wearð se gūðrinc: hē mid gāre stang
wlancne wīcing, þe him þā wunde forgeaf.
Frōd wæs se fyrdrinc; hē lēt his francan wadan
þurh ðæs hysses hals, hand wīsode 125
þæt hē on þām fǣrsceaðan feorh gerǣhte.
Ðā hē ōþerne ofstlīce scēat,
þæt sēo byrne tōbærst; hē wæs on brēostum wund
þurh ðā hringlocan, him æt heortan stōd
ǣtterne ord. Se eorl wæs þē blīþra: 130
hlōh þā mōdi man, sǣde Metode þanc
ðæs dægweorces þe him Drihten forgeaf.
Forlēt þā drenga sum daroð of handa,
flēogan of folman, þæt sē tō forð gewāt
þurh ðone æþelan Æþelrēdes þegen. 135
Him be healfe stōd hyse unweaxen,
cniht on gecampe, sē full cāflīce
brǣd of þām beorne blōdigne gār,
Wulfstānes bearn, Wulfmǣr se geonga;
forlēt forheardne faran eft ongēan; 140
ord in gewōd, þæt sē on eorþan læg,
þe his þēoden ǣr þearle gerǣhte.
Ēode þā gesyrwed secg tō þām eorle;
hē wolde þæs beornes bēagas gefeccan,
rēaf and hringas, and gerēnod swurd. 145
Ðā Byrhtnōð brǣd bill of scēðe
brād and brūnecg, and on þā byrnan slōh.

---

[13] *ceorle* This usually means 'freeman of the lowest class'; cf. 240, where an English *ceorl* adds his own heroic words and deeds to those of his aristocratic

106 *stemnetton* stood firm; *stīðhicgende* resolute
107 *hysas* young men; *hogodon* considered; *georne* eagerly
108 *hwā* who; *ǣrost* first, i.e. before anyone else
109 *on fǣgean men feorh* the life in a doomed man; *gewinnan* gain by fighting
110 *wigan* from a warrior; *wæl* the slain
111 *stædefæste* steadfast; *stihte* . . . Byrhtnoð exhorted them
112 *hyssa gehwylc* each of the young men; *hogode tō* should be intent on
113 *on Denon* among the Danes; *dōm* glory; *gefeohtan* win by fighting
114 *Wōd* advanced; *wīges heard* [one] hard in battle; *āhōf* raised
115 *tō gebeorge* as a defence; *wið* . . . stepped forward against the man, i.e. against Byrhtnoð
116 *Ēode* went; *swā ānrǣd* equally resolute; *ceorle* churl
117 *ǣgþer hyra* each of them; *ōðrum* . . . intended evil to the other
118 *sǣrinc* seaman; *sūþerne* [of] southern [make]
119 *gewundod* see 97; *wigena hlāford* the lord of warriors
120 *scēaf* thrust, i.e. against the spear that had struck him; *sceaft* shaft; *tōbærst* broke
121 *þæt* . . . [Byrhtnoð] broke (*sprengde*) the spear; *þæt* . . . so that it sprang back
122 *Gegremod* enraged; *gūðrinc* warrior; *stang* pierced
123 *wlancne* proud; *wunde* wound (G f: 5.5); *forgeaf* gave
124 *Frōd* experienced; *fyrdrinc* warrior; *lēt wadan* caused to go; *francan* spear
125 *þurh* through; *hals* neck; *hand wīsode* [his] hand guided [it]
126 *þæt* . . . so that he seized (*gerǣhte*) the life in the raider (*fǣrsceaðan*)
127 *ōþerne* a second [Viking]; *ofstlīce* quickly; *scēat* struck
128 *sēo byrne* the corslet; *brēostum* breast (lit. pl.); *wund* see 97
129 *hringlocan* linked rings, i.e. of the corslet; *him* . . . 'lodged in his heart'
130 *ǣtterne* deadly; *þē blīþra* the happier (5.10)
131 *hlōh* laughed; *mōdi* brave; *Metode* to God
132 *ðæs dægweorces* for the day's work (5.13); *him* to him; *Drihten* the Lord; *forgeaf* gave
133 *Forlēt flēogan* let fly; *drenga sum* one of the [Viking] warriors; *daroð* spear
134 *of folman* from his hand; *sē* it; *tō forð* too deeply; *gewāt* went
135 *ðone* . . . the noble thane of Æþelred
136 *Him be healfe* By his side (5.14); *unweaxen* immature
137 *cniht* youth; *gecampe* battle; *full* very; *cāflīce* bravely
138 *brǣd* plucked out; *blōdigne* bloody
139 *se geonga* the young
140 *forheardne* [a] very hard [weapon]
141 *in gewōd* went in; *sē* he, i.e. the Viking
142 *þe* . . . who had wounded (*ǣr gerǣhte*, 5.25) his prince sorely (*þearle*). The reference is to the Viking who had wounded Byrhtnoð
143 *gesyrwed secg* armed man
144 *bēagas* rings (see footnote 3); *gefeccan* seize
145 *rēaf* booty; *hringas* rings; *gerēnod* ornamented
146 *brǣd* drew; *bill* see 98; *of scēðe* from the sheath
147 *brād* broad; *brūnecg* bright-edged (5.35); *slōh* struck

---

companions. Here the word refers to one of the enemy force, and is doubtless used pejoratively.

Tō raþe hine gelette   lidmanna sum,
þā hē þæs eorles   earm āmyrde.
Fēoll þā tō foldan   fealohilte swurd: 150
ne mihte hē gehealdan   heardne mēce,
wǣpnes wealdan.   Þā gȳt þæt word gecwæð
hār hilderinc,   hyssas bylde,
bæd gangan forð   gōde gefēran.
Ne mihte þā on fōtum leng   fæste gestandan,   155
hē tō heofenum wlāt
'Ic þancige þē,   ðēoda Waldend,
ealra þǣra wynna   þe ic on worulde gebād.
Nū ic āh, milde Metod,   mǣste þearfe,
þæt þū mīnum gāste   gōdes geunne,   160
þæt mīn sāwul tō ðē   sīðian mōte,
on þīn geweald,   þēoden engla,
mid friþe ferian;   ic eom frymdi tō þē
þæt hī helsceaðan   hȳnan ne mōton.'
Ðā hine hēowon   hǣðene scealcas,   165
and bēgen þā beornas   þe him big stōdon,
Ælfnōð and Wulmǣr   bēgen lāgon,
ðā onemn hyra frēan   feorh gesealdon.
Hī bugon þā fram beaduwe   þe þǣr bēon noldon:
þǣr wurdon Oddan bearn   ǣrest on flēame,   170
Godrīc fram gūþe,   and þone gōdan forlēt,
þe him mænigne oft   mearh gesealde,
hē gehlēop þone eoh   þe āhte his hlāford,
on þām gerǣdum   þēh hit riht ne wæs,
and his brōðru mid him   bēgen ærndon,   175
Godwine and Godwīg,   gūþe ne gȳmdon,
ac wendon fram þām wīge,   and þone wudu sōhton,
flugon on þæt fæsten,   and hyra fēore burgon,
and manna mā   þonne hit ǣnig mǣð wǣre,
gyf hī þā geearnunga   ealle gemundon,   180
þe hē him tō duguþe   gedōn hæfde.
Swā him Offa on dæg   ǣr āsǣde,
on þām meþelstede,   þā hē gemōt hæfde,
þæt þǣr mōdiglīce   manega sprǣcon,
þe eft æt þearfe   þolian noldon.   185

Þā wearð āfeallen   þæs folces ealdor,
Æþelrēdes eorl.   Ealle gesāwon
heorðgenēatas   þæt hyra hearra læg.
Þā ðǣr wendon forð   wlance þegenas,
unearge men   efston georne: 190
hī woldon þā ealle   ōðer twēga,
līf forlǣtan   oððe lēofne gewrecan.
Swā hī bylde forð   bearn Ælfrīces,

148 *Tō raþe* too soon; *hine* . . . one of the sailors impeded (*gelette*) him
149 *þā* when; *earm* arm; *āmyrde* wounded
150 *fealohilte* yellow-hilted
151 *mēce* sword
152 *wealdan* see 67; *þā gȳt* still; *gecwæð* spoke
153 *hār* grey[-haired]; *hilderinc* warrior; *bylde* encouraged
154 *gefēran* comrades
155 *leng* longer (5.8); *gestandan* stand
156 *wlāt* looked
157 *þancige* thank; *ðēoda* of peoples; *Waldend* Ruler
158 *ealra* . . . for all of the joys; *gebād* have experienced
159 *āh mǣste þearfe* have most need; *milde* merciful
160 *mīnum gāste* to my spirit; *gōdes* well-being; *geunne* grant
161 *sāwul* soul; *sīðian mōte* may journey
162 *on* into; *geweald* power; *engla* of angels
163 *friþe* peace; *ferian* go; *ic* . . . I beseech thee
164 *hī* it, i.e. the soul (5.1,9); *helsceaðan* hell-fiends; *hȳnan* harm
165 *hǣðene* heathen; *scealcas* warriors
166 *bēgen* both; *big* = *bī* by
168 *onemn* beside; *frēan* lord; *gesealdon* gave up
169 *bugon* moved; *beaduwe* battle
170 *Oddan bearn* Odda's sons; *wurdon ǣrest on flēame* were first in flight
171 *þone* . . . abandoned the good [man]
172 *mænigne mearh* many a steed; *gesealde* gave
173 *gehlēop* leaped upon; *eoh* war-horse; *þe* . . . which his lord owned
174 *gerǣdum* trappings; *þēh* = *þēah* though; *riht* right
175 *brōðru* brothers; *ærndon* galloped
176 *gȳmdon* heeded
177 *wendon* turned; *wudu* wood; *sōhton* made for
178 *flugon* fled; *fæsten* fastness; *fēore* life; *burgon* saved (5.23)
179 *manna mā* more men (5.13); *mǣð* what is right; *þonne* . . . 'than was at all fitting'
180 *þā geearnunga ealle* all the favours; *gemundon* remembered
181 *him tō duguþe* for their benefit (5.14); *gedōn* done
182 *on dæg* on a day; *āsǣde* said
183 *meþelstede* meeting-place; *gemōt* council
184 *mōdiglīce* boldly; *sprǣcon* spoke
185 *eft* afterwards; *æt þearfe* at [a time of] need; *þolian* endure
186 *āfeallen* fallen; *ealdor* see 37
187 *ealle heorðgenēatas* all the hearth-comrades
188 *hearra* lord
189 *wendon* went; *wlance* proud; *þegenas* thanes
190 *unearge* undaunted; *efston* hastened
191 *hī* . . . then they all desired; *ōðer twēga* one of two [things]
192 *forlǣtan* to give up; *lēofne* the dear [one]; *gewrecan* avenge
193 *hī* them; *bylde forð* urged forward

wiga wintrum geong, wordum mǣlde,
Ælfwine þā cwæð (hē on ellen spræc): 195
'Gemunað þāra mǣla þe wē oft æt meodo sprǣcon,[14]
þonne wē on bence bēot āhōfon,
hæleð on healle, ymbe heard gewinn:
nū mæg cunnian hwā cēne sȳ.
Ic wylle mīne æþelo eallum gecȳþan, 200
þæt ic wæs on Myrcon miccles cynnes;
wæs mīn ealda fæder Ealhelm hāten,
wīs ealdorman, woruldgesǣlig.
Ne sceolon mē on þǣre þēode þegenas ætwītan,
þæt ic of ðisse fyrde fēran wille, 205
eard gesēcan, nū mīn ealdor ligeð
forhēawen æt hilde. Mē is þæt hearma mǣst:
hē wæs ǣgðer mīn mǣg and mīn hlāford.'
Þā hē forð ēode, fǣhðe gemunde,
þæt hē mid orde ānne gerǣhte 210
flotan on þām folce, þæt sē on foldan læg
forwegen mid his wǣpne. Ongan þā winas manian,
frȳnd and gefēran, þæt hī forð ēodon.
Offa gemǣlde, æscholt āsceōc:
'Hwæt þū, Ælfwine, hafast ealle gemanode, 215
þegenas tō þearfe. Nū ūre þēoden līð,
eorl on eorðan, ūs is eallum þearf
þæt ūre ǣghwylc ōþerne bylde
wigan tō wīge, þā hwīle þe hē wǣpen mæge
habban and healdan, heardne mēce, 220
gār and gōd swurd. Ūs Godrīc hæfð,
earh Oddan bearn, ealle beswicene:
wēnde þæs formoni man, þā hē on mēare rād,
on wlancan þām wicge, þæt wǣre hit ūre hlāford;
forþan wearð hēr on felda folc tōtwǣmed, 225
scyldburh tōbrocen. Ābrēoðe his angin,
þæt hē hēr swā manigne man āflȳmde.'
Lēofsunu gemǣlde, and his linde āhōf,
bord tō gebeorge, hē þām beorne oncwæð:
'Ic þæt gehāte, þæt ic heonon nelle 230
flēon fōtes trym, ac wille furðor gān,
wrecan on gewinne mīnne winedrihten.
Ne þurfon mē embe Stūrmere stedefæste hæleð

---

[14] Here, and in 184f. and 258, the reference is to the heroic custom of undertaking, formally and in public, to perform valiant deeds. Cf. 4.7.69 and 70. Tacitus says that banquets were often occasions for serious discussion: 'At no other time . . . is the heart so open to frank suggestions or so quick to

194 *wintrum geong* young in winters, i.e. years; *mǣlde* see 27
195 *on ellen* boldly
196 *gemunað* remember (5.23); *þāra mǣla* the times; *meodo* mead
197 *bence* bench; *āhōfon* raised up, 'uttered loudly'
198 *hæleð on healle* warriors in hall; *ymbe* about; *gewinn* battle
199 *nū* . . . now [anyone] may prove who is valiant (*cēne*)
200 *æþelo* noble breeding; *eallum* to all; *gecȳþan* declare
201 *on Myrcon* among the Mercians; *miccles cynnes* from a great family
202 *ealda fæder* grandfather
203 *wīs ealdorman* wise nobleman; *woruldgesǣlig* prosperous
204 *on þǣre þēode* among that people; *ætwītan* reproach
205 *of* from; *fyrde* army
206 *eard* homeland; *gesēcan* go to; *nū* now that
207 *forhēawen* see 99; *Mē* to me; *hearma* of sorrows; *mǣst* greatest
208 *ǣgðer* both; *mǣg* kinsman
209 *fǣhðe* of vengeance; *gemunde* was mindful
210 *þæt* so that; *orde* see 94; *ānne flotan* one sailor; *gerǣhte* see 142
211 *flotan* see 56; *on* among
212 *forwegen* killed; *winas* comrades; *Ongan manian* exhorted
213 *frȳnd* friends; *gefēran* companions
214 *gemǣlde* spoke; *æscholt* ash-wood [spear]; *āsceōc* shook
215 *Hwæt* Oh!; *gemanode* exhorted
216 *tō þearfe* needfully; *Nū* Now that
217 *ūs* . . . [there] is need for all of us
218 *ūre ǣghwylc* each of us; *ōþerne bylde* should encourage the other
219 *wigan* warrior
220 *mēce* sword
221 *hæfð beswicene* has betrayed (5.25)
222 *earh* cowardly
223 *wēnde* thought; *þæs* anticipates *þæt*, 224; *formoni man* very many a man; *mēare* steed; *rād* see 2
224 *on* . . . on the proud horse
225 *forþan* for that [reason]; *felda* field; *tōtwǣmed* divided
226 *scyldburh* shield-wall; *tōbrocen* smashed (5.36); *Ābrēoðe* . . . May his plan perish
227 *āflȳmde* caused to flee
228 *gemǣlde* see 214; *linde* see 83
229 *gebeorge* see 115; *þām beorne* to the man; *oncwæð* replied
230 *gehāte* promise; *heonon nelle* will not [go] hence (5.20)
231 *flēon* see 178; *fōtes trym* the space of a foot; *furðor* further
232 *winedrihten* friend [and] lord
233 *þurfon* see 18; *embe* round about; *Stūrmere*, i.e. Leofsunu's home; *stedefæste* see 111

---

warm to a great appeal' (*Germania*, ch. 22). *Bēot* may be translated as 'boast' or 'vow', but neither word is quite satisfactory; 'challenge' is appropriate in 11, since at that point a Viking is speaking.

wordum ætwītan, nū mīn wine gecranc,
þæt ic hlāfordlēas hām sīðie, 235
wende fram wīge; ac mē sceal wǣpen niman,
ord and īren.' Hē ful yrre wōd,
feaht fæstlīce, flēam hē forhogode.
Dunnere þā cwæð, daroð ācwehte,
unorne ceorl, ofer eall clypode, 240
bæd þæt beorna gehwylc Byrhtnōð wrǣce:
'Ne mæg nā wandian sē þe wrecan þenceð
frēan on folce, nē for fēore murnan.'
Þā hī forð ēodon, fēores hī ne rōhton;
ongunnon þā hīredmen heardlīce feohtan, 245
grame gārberend, and God bǣdon
þæt hī mōston gewrecan hyra winedrihten,
and on hyra fēondum fyl gewyrcan.
Him se gȳsel[15] ongan geornlīce fylstan;
hē wæs on Norðhymbron heardes cynnes, 250
Ecglāfes bearn, him wæs Æscferð nama.
Hē ne wandode nā æt þām wīgplegan,
ac hē fȳsde forð flān geneahhe;
hwīlon hē on bord scēat, hwīlon beorn tǣsde,
ǣfre embe stunde hē sealde sume wunde, 255
þā hwīle ðe hē wǣpna wealdan mōste.
Þā gȳt on orde stōd Ēadweard se langa,
gearo and geornful; gylpwordum spræc,
þæt hē nolde flēogan fōtmǣl landes,
ofer bæc būgan, þā his betera leg. 260
Hē bræc þone bordweall, and wið ðā beornas feaht,
oð þæt hē his sincgyfan on þām sǣmannum
wurðlīce wrec ǣr hē on wæle lǣge.
Swā dyde Æþerīc, æþele gefēra,
fūs and forðgeorn, feaht eornoste, 265
Sībyrhtes brōðor, and swīðe mænig ōþer
clufon cellod bord, cēne hī weredon;
bærst bordes lærig, and sēo byrne sang
gryrelēoða sum. Þā æt gūðe slōh
Offa þone sǣlidan, þæt hē on eorðan fēoll, 270
and ðǣr Gaddes mǣg grund gesōhte:
raðe wearð æt hilde Offa forhēawen.
Hē hæfde ðēah geforþod þæt hē his frēan gehēt,
swā hē bēotode ǣr wið his bēahgifan,

---

[15] *Se gȳsel* The hostage is from Northumbria, a part of England largely occupied by the Scandinavians. It was customary for such hostages to fight alongside their 'hosts'.

234 *gecranc* has fallen
235 *hlāfordlēas* lordless; *hām* homewards; *sīðie* see 161
236 *wende* turn
237 *īren* iron; *yrre* see 28
238 *flēam* see 170; *fæstlīce* see 66; *forhogode* scorned
239 *daroð* see 133; *ācwehte* shook
240 *unorne* humble; *ceorl* see 116; *clypode* see 9
241 *wrǣce* avenge (5.27)
242 *Ne* . . . He can never flinch (*wandian*) who intends to avenge
243 *frēan* see 168; *on folce* among the people; *nē* . . . nor be concerned about life
244 *rōhton* cared about (5.23)
245 *hīredmen* household retainers; *heardlīce* fiercely
246 *grame gārberend* fierce spear-bearers; *bǣdon* asked
247 *gewrecan* see 192
248 *fyl* death; *gewyrcan* bring about
249 *Him* them; *gȳsel* hostage; *geornlīce* eagerly; *fylstan* to help
250 *on Norðhymbron* among the Northumbrians; *heardes cynnes* from a brave family
251 *nama* name
252 *wīgplegan* battle-play
253 *fȳsde* shot; *flān* arrows; *geneahhe* frequently
254 *scēat* see 127; *hwīlon* at times; *tǣsde* lacerated
255 *ǣfre* constantly; *embe stunde* 'at short intervals'; *sealde* gave; *wunde* see 123
256 *wealdan* see 67
257 *gȳt* see 152; *on orde* in the front line; *se langa* the tall
258 *gearo* see 56; *geornful* eager; *gylpwordum* with vows (see footnote 14)
259 *fōtmǣl landes* a foot of ground
260 *ofer bæc* backwards; *būgan* move; *betera* superior
261 *bræc* broke; *bordweall* the shield-wall
262 *sincgyfan* treasure-giver, i.e. Byrhtnoð; *sǣmannum* see 22
263 *wurðlīce* honourably; *wrec* = *wræc* avenged; *on wæle* among the dead
264 *Swā* Likewise; *dyde* did; *æþele* see 135
265 *fūs* ready; *forðgeorn* 'eager to advance'; *feaht* fought; *eornoste* resolutely
266 *brōðor* see 175
267 *clufon* split; *cellod* with boss; *cēne* see 199; *hī weredon* defended themselves
268 *bærst* clashed; *lærig* ?rim; *byrne* see 128
269 *gryrelēoða sum* a terrible song (5.13); *æt gūðe* in the battle; *slōh* . . . Offa struck the seafarer
271 *mǣg* see 208; *grund gesōhte* sought the ground, i.e. was struck down
272 *raðe* soon; *forhēawen* see 99
273 *ðēah* however; *geforþod* accomplished; *þæt* . . . what he had promised his lord
274 *swā* as; *bēotode* vowed; *bēahgifan* ring-giver

þæt hī sceoldon bēgen on burh[16] rīdan, 275
hāle tō hāme, oððe on here crincgan,
on wælstōwe wundum sweltan.
Hē læg ðegenlīce ðēodne gehende.
Ðā wearð borda gebræc; brimmen wōdon,
gūðe gegremode; gār oft þurhwōd 280
fǣges feorhhūs. Forð þā ēode Wīstān,
Þurstānes sunu, wið þās secgas feaht;
hē wæs on geþrange hyra þrēora bana,
ǣr him Wīgelmes bearn on þām wæle lǣge.
Þǣr wæs stīð gemōt: stōdon fæste 285
wigan on gewinne; wīgend cruncon,
wundum wērige; wæl fēol on eorþan.
Ōswold and Ealdwold ealle hwīle,
bēgen þā gebrōþru, beornas trymedon,
hyra winemāgas wordon bǣdon 290
þæt hī þǣr æt ðearfe þolian sceoldon,
unwāclīce wǣpna nēotan.
Byrhtwold maþelode, bord hafenode,
sē wæs eald genēat, æsc ācwehte,
hē ful baldlīce beornas lǣrde: 295
'Hige sceal þē heardra, heorte þē cēnre,
mōd sceal þē māre, þē ūre mægen lȳtlað.
Hēr līð ūre ealdor eall forhēawen,
gōd on grēote; ā mæg gnornian
sē ðe nū fram þīs wīgplegan wendan þenceð. 300
Ic eom frōd fēores. Fram ic ne wille,
ac ic mē be healfe mīnum hlāforde
be swā lēofan men licgan þence.'

---

16 *burh* This may refer to the fortified town of Maldon; or to Byrhtnoð's own (fortified) place of residence.

275 *bēgen* see 166; *on burh* to the stronghold
276 *hāle* unhurt; *here* battle; *crincgan* die
277 *wælstōwe* see 79; *wundum sweltan* die of wounds
278 *ðegenlīce* in a thane-like way, nobly; *gehende* beside
279 *borda gebræc* clash of shields; *brimmen* seamen
280 *gūðe gegremode* enraged by battle; *þurhwōd* pierced
281 *fǣges* of the doomed; *feorhhūs* life-house, i.e. body (5.35)
282 *sunu* see 60; *secgas* men
283 *geþrange* throng; *hyra þrēora* of three of them; *bana* the killer
284 *ǣr* before; *him lǣge* lay (5.23,27); *Wīgelmes bearn* Wigelm's son – possibly Offa (272)
285 *stīð* hard; *gemōt* encounter
286 *wigan* warriors; *wīgend* warriors; *cruncon* fell
287 *wērige* exhausted
289 *gebrōþru* brothers; *trymedon* rallied
290 *bǣdon hyra winemāgas* exhorted their beloved kinsmen; *wordon* = *wordum*
291 *æt ðearfe þolian* see 185
292 *unwāclīce* not weakly; *nēotan* use
293 *maþelode* see 26; *hafenode* see 26
294 *eald genēat* long-serving retainer; *æsc* see 27; *ācwehte* see 239
295 *baldlīce* boldly; *lǣrde* exhorted
296 *Hige* Mind; *sceal* must [be] (5.20); *þē heardra* the more resolute (5.8,10); *cēnre* more valiant
297 *mōd* spirit; *þē māre* the greater; *þē* as (5.28); *mægen* [bodily] strength; *lȳtlað* lessens
298 *līð* lies; *ealdor* see 37
299 *gōd* the good [man]; *grēote* dust; *ā* ever; *mæg gnornian* he can mourn
300 *þīs* = *þȳs* (5.6,10); *wendan* see 236
301 *frōd fēores* advanced in life; *Fram* away; *ic . . .* I will not [go] (5.20)
302 *healfe* see 136
303 *be . . .* beside so dear a man; *licgan þence* intend to lie

4.2 The Fall of the Angels

Fēollon þā ufon of heofnum
þurh swā longe swā þrēo niht and dagas
þā englas of heofnum on helle, and hēo ealle forsceōp
Drihten tō dēoflum. Forþon hēo his dǣd and word
noldon weorðian, forþon hē hēo on wyrse lēoht[1] 5
under eorðan neoðan ælmihtig God
sette sigelēase on þā sweartan helle.
Þǣr hæbbað hēo on ǣfyn ungemet lange
ealra fēonda gehwilc fȳr ednēowe.
Þonne cymð on ūhtan ēasterne wind, 10
forst fyrnum cald; symble fȳr oððe gār,[2]
sum heard geþwing habban sceoldon.
Worhte man hit him tō wīte (hyra woruld wæs gehwyrfed)
forman sīðe fylde helle
mid þām andsacum. Hēoldon englas forð 15
heofonrīces hēhðe, þe ǣr Godes hyldo gelǣston.
Lāgon þā ōðre fȳnd on þām fȳre, þe ǣr swā feala hæfdon
gewinnes wið heora Waldend; wīte þoliað,
hātne heaðowelm helle tōmiddes,
brand and brāde līgas, swilce ēac þā biteran rēcas, 20
þrosm and þȳstro, forþon hīe þegnscipe[3]
Godes forgȳmdon. Hīe hyra gāl beswāc,
engles oferhygd: noldon Alwaldan
word weorþian; hæfdon wīte micel,
wǣron þā befeallene fȳre tō botme 25
on þā hātan helle, þurh hygelēaste
and þurh ofermētto. Sōhton ōþer land,
þæt wæs lēohtes lēas and wæs līges full,
fȳres fǣr micel. Fȳnd ongēaton
þæt hīe hæfdon gewrixled wīta unrīm, 30
þurh heora miclan mōd, and þurh miht Godes,
and þurh ofermētto ealra swīðost.
Þā spræc se ofermōda cyning þe ǣr wæs engla scȳnost,
hwītost on heofne and his Hearran lēof,
Drihtne dȳre, oð hīe tō dole wurdon, 35
þæt him for gālscipe God sylfa wearð
mihtig on mōde yrre, wearp hine on þæt morðer innan,

This passage is from a poem of nearly 3000 lines in one of the four codices discussed in 1.5, the Junius Manuscript. It is basically a paraphrase of Genesis. Our extract (ll. 306–74) is from a part which is a translation from an Old Saxon poem. Its themes – the creation, the defeat of Satan, and the story of Adam and Eve – are treated somewhat similarly elsewhere, e.g. by Ælfric in the first of the Catholic Homilies, as well as by Milton in *Paradise Lost.*

1 *ufon* from above; *of* from
2 *þurh . . .* for as long as three nights and days
3 *on helle* into hell; *hēo* them; *forsceōp* transformed
4 *Drihten* Lord; *tō dēoflum* into devils; *Forþon* Because (5.28); *hēo* they; *dǣd* deed
5 *weorðian* honour; *forþon* therefore; *hē* i.e. God; *wyrse lēoht* worse light, i.e. gloom (but see footnote 1)
6 *neoðan* beneath; *ælmihtig* almighty
7 *sette* placed; *sigelēase* defeated; *sweartan* black
8 *ǣfyn* evening; *ungemet* excessively
9 *fēonda* devils; *gehwilc* each; *ednēowe* renewed
10 *cymð* comes; *on ūhtan* at daybreak; *ēasterne* eastern
11 *forst* frost; *fyrnum* extremely; *symble* continually; *oððe* or
12 *geþwing* torment; *sceoldon* were obliged
13 *Worhte . . .* A state of torment (*wīte*) was created for them (5.26); *gehwyrfed* overturned
14 *forman sīðe* for the first time; *fylde . . .* hell was filled (5.26)
15 *andsacum* adversaries; *forð* thenceforth
16 *heofonrīces* of the kingdom of heaven; *hēhðe* the highest point; *ǣr gelǣston* had achieved (5.25); *hyldo* favour
17 *lāgon* lay; *þā ōðre* the others; *fȳnd* the fiends; *swā feala gewinnes* so much strife
18 *Waldend* Ruler; *þoliað* suffer
19 *hātne* hot; *heaðowelm* fierce surge of flame; *tōmiddes* amidst
20 *brand* fire; *brāde* broad; *līgas* flames; *swilce ēac* so also; *biteran* bitter; *rēcas* fumes
21 *þrosm* smoke; *þȳstro* darkness; *þegnscipe* service
22 *forgȳmdon* neglected; *hīe* them; *gāl* folly; *beswāc* led astray
23 *engles* of the angel, i.e. Satan; *oferhygd* pride; *Alwaldan* of the Almighty
24 *weorþian* see 5
25 *befeallene* fallen; *botme* bottom
26 *hygelēaste* heedlessness
27 *ofermētto* pride
28 *lēohtes lēas* deprived of light
29 *fǣr* peril; *ongēaton* realized
30 *gewrixled* got in exchange; *wīta unrīm* countless punishments (5.13)
31 *mōd* pride; *miht* the might
32 *ealra swīðost* most of all
33 *ofermōda* arrogant; *scȳnost* brightest
34 *hwītost* whitest; *his . . .* dear to his Lord
35 *dȳre* dear; *oð* until; *hīe* i.e. the fallen angels; *tō dole wurdon* became foolish
36 *þæt* so that; *him . . .* because of their folly; *God . . .* mighty God himself became angry in his heart
37 *mihtig* mighty; *wearp* threw; *hine* i.e. Satan; *on innan* into; *morðer* torment

---

[1] *lēoht* It may be that *lēoht* here means 'world', as was possible in Old Saxon.
[2] *gār* The ordinary sense 'spear' is perhaps used in this context to imply 'piercing cold'.
[3] The relationship between Satan (with his followers) and God is seen as similar to that of the 'hearth-troop' and Byrhtnoð in 4.1.

niðer on þæt nīobedd, and sceōp him naman siððan,
cwæð se hēhsta hātan sceolde
Sātan siððan, hēt hine þǣre sweartan helle 40
grundes gȳman, nalles wið God winnan.
Sātan maðelode,[4] sorgiende spræc,
sē ðe helle forð healdan sceolde,
gīeman þæs grundes, wæs ǣr Godes engel
hwīt on heofne, oð hine his hyge forspēon 45
and his ofermētto ealra swīðost,
þæt hē ne wolde wereda Drihtnes
word wurðian. Wēoll him on innan
hyge ymb his heortan, hāt wæs him ūtan
wrāðlic wīte; hē þā worde cwæð: 50
'Is þes ænga styde ungelīc swīðe
þām ōðrum þe wē ǣr cūðon,
hēan on heofonrīce, þe mē mīn Hearra onlāg,
þēah wē hine for þām Alwaldan āgan ne mōston,
rōmigan ūres rīces. Næfð hē þēah riht gedōn 55
þæt hē ūs hæfð befælled fȳre tō botme,
helle þǣre hātan, heofonrīce benumen,
hafað hit gemearcod mid moncynne
tō gesettanne. Þæt mē is sorga mǣst
þæt Ādām sceal, þe wæs of eorðan geworht, 60
mīnne stronglican stōl behealdan,
wesan him on wynne, and wē þis wīte þolien,
hearm on þisse helle. Wālā! Āhte ic mīnra handa geweald,
and mōste āne tīd ūte weorðan,
wesan āne winterstunde,[5] þonne ic mid þȳs werode –[6] 65
ac licgað mē ymbe īrenbenda,
rīdeð racentan sāl. Ic eom rīces lēas:
habbað mē swā hearde helle clommas
fæste befangen.

---

[4] *Sātan maðelode* Cf. 4.1.26, 293 for this 'formula'.
[5] *winterstunde* A 'winter-hour' is an hour of minimum length, since the day from sunrise to sunset was divided into twelve equal periods.
[6] *þȳs werode* Satan appears to break off here in despair.

38 *niðer* down; *nīobedd* corpse-bed, i.e. hell; *sceōp* created; *him* for him; *naman* name; *siððan* afterwards
39 *se hēhsta* the highest, i.e. God; *hātan sceolde* he should be called (5.26)
40 *þǣre* . . . of that black hell
41 *grundes* abyss; *gȳman* take charge of; *nalles* not at all; *winnan* to struggle
42 *maðelode* spoke; *sorgiende* sorrowing
43 *forð* henceforth
44 *gīeman* see 41
45 *forspēon* led astray
47 *wereda Drihtnes* of the Lord of troops
48 *wurðian* see 5; *Wēoll* surged
49 *hāt* . . . *wīte* the severe (*wrāðlic*) torment was hot around him
50 *þā* then
51 *Is* . . . This narrow (*ænga*) place is; *ungelīc* unlike
53 *hēan* high; *onlāg* granted
54 *hine* it, i.e. the high place; *for* because of; *āgan* have; *ne mōston* were not able to
55 *rōmigan* to strive for; *rīces* kingdom; *næfð* has not (5.30); *riht* right
56 *þæt* 'inasmuch as'; *befælled* cast down; *fȳr* . . . see 25
57 *benumen* deprived of
58 *hafað hit gemearcod* he has designated it; *moncynne* mankind
59 *tō gesettanne* to be peopled (5.26); *sorga mǣst* the greatest of sorrows
60 *sceal behealdan* is to occupy; *geworht* made
61 *stronglican* powerful; *stōl* throne
62 *wesan him* exist (5.14); *on wynne* in joy; *þolien* suffer (5.27)
63 *hearm* grief; *Wālā* Alas; *Āhte* . . . If I had the power of my hands
64 *mōste ūte weorðan* might get outside; *āne tīd* one hour (5.12)
65 *wesan* be [outside]; *winterstunde* winter-hour; *werode* troop
66 *licgað* . . . iron bonds are lying around me (5.24)
67 *rīdeð* is riding [on me]; *racentan* of the fetter; *sāl* the bond
68 *habbað befangen* have caught; *hearde* strongly; *helle clommas* the bonds of hell

4·3 The Dream of the Rood

Hwæt, ic swefna cyst   secgan wylle,
hwæt mē gemǣtte   tō midre nihte,
syðþan reordberend   reste wunedon.
Þūhte mē þæt ic gesāwe   syllicre trēow
on lyft lǣdan   lēohte bewunden,   5
bēama beorhtost.   Eall þæt bēacen wæs
begoten mid golde;   gimmas stōdon
fægere æt foldan scēatum,[1]   swylce þǣr fīfe wǣron
uppe on þām eaxlgespanne.   Behēoldon þær engeldryhta feala
fægere þurh forðgesceaft;   ne wæs ðǣr hūru fracodes gealga,   10
ac hine þǣr behēoldon   hālige gāstas,
men ofer moldan,   and eall þēos mǣre gesceaft.
  Syllic wæs se sigebēam,   and ic synnum fāh,
forwundod mid wommum.   Geseah ic wuldres trēow
wǣdum geweorðod[2]   wynnum scīnan,   15
gegyred mid golde;   gimmas hæfdon
bewrigen weorðlīce   Wealdendes trēow.
Hwæðre ic þurh þæt gold   ongytan meahte
earmra ǣrgewin,   þæt hit ǣrest ongan
swǣtan on þā swīðran healfe.   Eall ic wæs mid sorgum gedrēfed,   20
forht ic wæs for þǣre fægran gesyhðe;   geseah ic þæt fūse bēacen
wendan wǣdum and blēom:[3]   hwīlum hit wæs mid wǣtan bestēmed,
beswyled mid swātes gange,   hwīlum mid since gegyrwed.
  Hwæðre ic þǣr licgende   lange hwīle
behēold hrēowcearig   Hǣlendes trēow,   25
oð ðæt ic gehȳrde   þæt hit hlēoðrode;
ongan þā word sprecan   wudu sēlesta:
  'Þæt wæs geāra iū   (ic þæt gȳta geman)
þæt ic wæs āhēawen   holtes on ende,
āstyred of stefne mīnum.   Genāman mē ðǣr strange fēondas,   30
geworhton him þǣr tō wæfersȳne,   hēton mē heora wergas hebban;
bǣron mē þǣr beornas on eaxlum,   oð ðæt hīe mē on beorg āsetton;
gefæstnodon mē þǣr fēondas genōge.   Geseah ic þā Frēan mancynnes
efstan elne micle,   þæt hē mē wolde on gestīgan.
Þǣr ic þā ne dorste   ofer Dryhtnes word   35

The Dream of the Rood is in the Vercelli Book, but a few fragments of the poem are inscribed in runic letters on the Ruthwell Cross, a stone monument dating from about 700. It is therefore possible either that the poem (or part of it) was in existence at that time, or that the inscriptions on this cross helped to inspire the work of a later poet. The whole poem consists of 156 lines, of which we give ll. 1–74. In the remainder, the cross addresses the dreamer, commanding him to describe his vision and its significance to other men. The narrator ends with an expression of his faith, and of his hope for life after death.

1 *Hwæt* Oh; *ic secgan wylle* I want to tell; *swefna* of dreams; *cyst* the best

2 *hwæt* what; *mē gemǣtte* I dreamed (5.22); *tō midre nihte* at midnight

3 *syðþan* when; *reordberend* speech-bearers, i.e. men; *reste* at rest; *wunedon* stayed, i.e. were

4 *þūhte mē* (5.22); *syllicre* wonderful, lit. more wonderful; *trēow* tree

5 *on lyft* aloft; *lǣdan* to be borne (5.24,26); *lēohte* with light; *bewunden* enveloped

6 *bēama* of trees; *beorhtost* brightest; *bēacen* beacon

7 *begoten* covered; *gimmas* gems; *stōdon* stood

8 *fægere* beautiful; *æt scēatum* at the corners; *swylce* likewise; *fīfe* five

9 *uppe* up; *eaxlgespanne* cross-beam; *Behēoldon* gazed; *engeldryhta* angel-hosts

10 *þurh forðgesceaft* 'for all time'; *hūru* indeed; *fracodes* of a vile [one]; *gealga* gallows

11 *hine . . .* beheld it there; *hālige* holy; *gāstas* spirits

12 *ofer* all over; *moldan* the earth; *þēos mǣre gesceaft* this glorious creation

13 *sigebēam* victory-tree; *synnum* with sins; *fāh* stained

14 *forwundod* severely wounded; *wommum* with sins; *wuldres* of glory

15 *wǣdum* with coverings; *geweorðod* adorned; *wynnum* beautifully (5.14); *scīnan* shine (5.24)

16 *gegyred* adorned

17 *bewrigen* covered; *weorðlīce* splendidly; *Wealdendes* Ruler's

18 *Hwæðre* Yet; *ongytan* perceive

19 *earmra* of the wretched; *ǣrgewin* former struggle

20 *swǣtan* to bleed; *swīðran* right; *sorgum* sorrows; *gedrēfed* troubled

21 *forht* afraid; *for* before; *gesyhðe* vision; *fūse* ready

22 *wendan* change; *blēom* in colours; *wǣtan* moisture; *bestēmed* drenched

23 *beswyled* soaked; *swātes gange* the flow of blood; *since* treasure; *gegyrwed* see 16

24 *licgende* lying

25 *hrēowcearig* sorrowful; *Hǣlendes* the Saviour's

26 *oð ðæt* until; *hlēoðrode* spoke

27 *wudu sēlesta* the best [piece of] wood

28 *geāra iū* long ago; *gȳta* still; *geman* remember

29 *āhēawen* hewn down; *holtes on ende* at the edge of the wood

30 *āstyred* moved; *stefne* root; *Genāman* seized (5.11); *strange* strong

31 *geworhton . . .* there they made [me] into a spectacle for themselves (*him*); *hēton . . .* they commanded me to lift up (*hebban*) their criminals

32 *eaxlum* shoulders; *beorg* hill; *āsetton* placed

33 *gefæstnodon* fastened; *genōge* enough; *Frēan* the Lord; *mancynnes* of mankind

34 *efstan* hasten; *elne mycle* with great zeal; *þæt* [I saw] that; *gestīgan* mount

35 *dorste* dared; *ofer* against; *Dryhtnes* Lord's

---

[1] *æt foldan scēatum* *Scēat* may mean either 'corner' or 'surface'; cf. 37. Probably the poet is here visualizing the cross as filling the sky and stretching from horizon to horizon.

[2] *wǣdum geweorðod* The reference of *wǣdum* may be to the ritual veiling of the cross on Good Friday. Another suggestion is that the poet is thinking of the Christian military standards of the Emperor Constantine, which had richly decorated banners attached to them. In the Good Friday hymn *Vexilla Regis*, the cross is described as 'adorned with royal purple'.

[3] *wendan wǣdum and blēom* This may be descriptive of the various colours of crosses carried at church services at different times in the liturgical year.

būgan oððe berstan, þā ic bifian geseah
eorðan scēatas.[4] Ealle ic mihte
fēondas gefyllan, hwæðre ic fæste stōd.[5]
Ongyrede hine þā geong hæleð, þæt wæs God ælmihtig,
strang and stīðmōd; gestāh hē on gealgan hēanne, 40
mōdig on manigra gesyhðe, þā hē wolde mancyn lȳsan.
Bifode ic þā mē se beorn ymbclypte; ne dorste ic hwæðre būgan tō
eorðan,
feallan tō foldan scēatum, ac ic sceolde fæste standan.
Rōd wæs ic āræ̅red, āhōf ic rīcne cyning,
heofona hlāford, hyldan mē ne dorste. 45
Þurhdrifan hī mē mid deorcan næglum; on mē syndon þā dolg
gesīene,
opene inwidhlemmas; ne dorste ic hira ǣnigum sceððan.
Bysmeredon hīe unc būtū ætgædere; eall ic wæs mid blōde
bestēmed,
begoten of þæs guman sīdan, siððan hē hæfde his gāst onsended.
'Feala ic on þām beorge gebiden hæbbe 50
wrāðra wyrda: geseah ic weruda God
þearle þenian; þȳstro hæfdon
bewrigen mid wolcnum Wealdendes hrǣw,
scīrne scīman; sceadu forð ēode,
wann under wolcnum.[6] Wēop eal gesceaft, 55
cwīðdon cyninges fyll: Crīst wæs on rōde.
Hwæðere þǣr fūse feorran cwōman
tō þām æðelinge; ic þæt eall behēold.
Sāre ic wæs mid sorgum gedrēfed, hnāg ic hwæðre þām secgum
tō handa
ēaðmōd elne mycle. Genāmon hīe þǣr ælmihtigne God, 60
āhōfon hine of ðām hefian wīte; forlēton mē þā hilderincas
standan stēame bedrifenne; eall ic wæs mid strǣlum[7] forwundod.
Ālēdon hīe hine limwērigne, gestōdon him æt his līces hēafdum;
behēoldon hīe ðǣr heofenes Dryhten, and hē hine ðǣr hwīle reste
mēðe æfter ðām miclan gewinne. Ongunnon him þā moldern
wyrcan 65
beornas on banan gesyhðe, curfon hīe ðæt of beorhtan stāne;
gesetton hīe ðǣron sigora Wealdend. Ongunnon him þā sorhlēoð
galan
earme on þā ǣfentīde, þā hīe woldon eft sīðian
mēðe fram þām mǣran þēodne; reste hē ðǣr mǣte weorode.[8]
Hwæðere wē ðǣr grēotende gōde hwīle 70
stōdon on staðole; stefn up gewāt
hilderinca; hrǣw cōlode,
fǣger feorgbold. Þā ūs man fyllan ongan
ealle tō eorðan; þæt wæs egeslic wyrd!

36 *būgan* bend; *berstan* break; *bifian* tremble
37 *scēatas* surfaces; *mihte gefyllan* could have felled
38 *hwæðre* see 18
39 *Ongyrede hine* stripped himself; *geong hæleð* young man; *ælmihtig* almighty
40 *stīðmōd* firm-minded (5.35); *gestāh* see 34; *hēanne* high
41 *mōdig* brave; *on gesyhðe* in the sight; *manigra* of many; *lȳsan* redeem
42 *Bifode* see 36; *ymbclypte* embraced
44 *Rōd* cross; *ārǣred* raised up; *āhōf* lifted up; *rīcne* powerful
45 *hyldan* bend
46 *Þurhdrifan* (5.11) pierced; *deorcan* (5.11) dark; *næglum* nails; *dolg* wounds; *gesīene* visible
47 *opene* open; *inwidhlemmas* malicious blows; *sceððan* injure (5.23)
48 *Bysmeredon* insulted; *unc* us two (5.9); *būtū* both; *ætgædere* together; *blōde* blood
49 *begoten* poured out; *of* from; *guman sīdan* man's side; *siððan* when; *onsended* sent forth
50 *gebiden* experienced
51 *wrāðra wyrda* cruel events; *weruda* of troops
52 *þearle* severely; *þenian* stretched out (5.26); *þȳstro* darkness
53 *bewrigen* covered; *wolcnum* clouds; *Wealdendes* see 17; *hrǣw* corpse
54 *scīrne* bright; *scīman* radiance; *sceadu* shadow
55 *wann* dark; *Wēop* wept; *gesceaft* see 12
56 *cwīðdon* . . . they, i.e. all created things, lamented; *fyll* fall
57 *fūse* eager [ones]; *feorran* from afar
58 *æðelinge* prince
59 *Sāre* sorely; *sorgum* . . . see 20; *hnāg* bent; *þām* . . . 'to the men's hands' (5.14)
60 *ēaðmōd* humble; *elne mycle* see 34
61 *hefian* heavy; *wīte* torment; *forlēton* left; *hilderincas* warriors
62 *stēame* moisture; *bedrifenne* drenched; *strǣlum* arrows
63 *Ālēdon* laid; *limwērigne* limb-weary; *gestōdon* stood; *him æt hēafdum* at his head (5.14); *his līces* of his body
64 *hine reste* rested himself
65 *mēðe* exhausted; *Ongunnon wyrcan* They made (5.24); *moldern* tomb
66 *on banan gesyhðe* in the sight of the slayer, i.e. the cross; *curfon* carved; *beorhtan* see 6; *stāne* stone
67 *sigora* of victories; *Ongunnon galan* They sang (5.24); *sorhlēoð* a song of sorrow
68 *earme* wretched [ones]; *ǣfentīde* evening; *sīðian* go
69 *mǣran* see 12; *mǣte weorode* 'alone' (see footnote 8)
70 *wē* i.e. the three crosses; *grēotende* weeping
71 *staðole* position; *stefn* voice
72 *cōlode* cooled
73 *fǣger* fair; *feorgbold* life-dwelling, i.e. body
74 *egeslic* fearful; *wyrd* fate

---

[4] Cf. Matthew 27,51 'And behold . . . the earth shook, and the rocks were split'.

[5] The cross presents itself as a loyal 'retainer' of Christ, ironically compelled to assist at his death instead of defending him.

[6] Cf. Matthew 27,45 'Now from the sixth hour there was darkness over all the land until the ninth hour'.

[7] *strǣlum* These are presumably the nails of 46; the use of a word meaning 'arrows' is appropriate in this context: the cross is a participant in Christ's 'battle'.

[8] *mǣte weorode* Literally this means 'with a poor-sized company'. This kind of understatement is a fairly common feature of OE style; cf. *genōge* 33, which clearly has the sense of 'many'.

4.4 The Rebirth of the Phoenix

Þǣr hē sylf biereð
in þæt trēow innan   torhte frætwe;
þǣr se wilda fugel   in þām wēstenne
ofer hēanne bēam   hūs getimbreð
wlitig ond wynsum,   ond gewīcað þǣr   5
sylf in þām solere,   ond ymbseteð ūtan
in þām lēafsceade   līc ond feþre
on healfa gehwāre   hālgum stencum[1]
ond þām æþelestum   eorþan blēdum.
Siteð sīþes fūs.   Þonne swegles gim,[2]   10
on sumeres tīd   sunne hātost
ofer sceadu scīneð   ond gesceapu drēogeð,
woruld geondwlīteð,   þonne weorðeð his
hūs onhǣted   þurh hādor swegl.
Wyrta wearmiað,   willsele stȳmeð   15
swētum swæccum,   þonne on swole byrneð
þurh fȳres feng   fugel mid neste.[3]
Bǣl bið onǣled.   Þonne brond þeceð
heoredrēorges hūs,   hrēoh ōnetteð,
fealo līg feormað,   ond fenix byrneð   20
fyrngēarum frōd;   þonne fȳr þigeð
lǣnne līchoman;   līf bið on sīðe,
fǣges feorhhord,   þonne flǣsc ond bān
ādlēg ǣleð.   Hwæþre him eft cymeð
æfter fyrstmearce   feorh ednīwe,   25
siþþan þā yslan   eft onginnað
æfter līgþræce   lūcan tōgædre
geclungne tō clēowenne.   Þonne clǣne bið
beorhtast nesta,   bǣle forgrunden
heaþorōfes hof.   Hrā bið ācōlad,   30
bānfæt gebrocen   ond se bryne sweþrað.
Þonne of þām āde   æples gelīcnes
on þǣre ascan bið   eft gemēted,
of þām weaxeð wyrm[4]   wundrum fǣger,
swylce hē of ǣgerum   ūt ālǣde,   35
scīr of scylle.

The Phoenix is a poem of 677 lines in the Exeter Book, the first part of which (including our extract, ll. 199–234) is a free translation of a Latin work ascribed to Lactantius (died c. AD 340). In Egyptian myths of the Creation, the phoenix was associated with the sun and with renewal, but the story of its rebirth through fire became popular as a Christian allegory and this is represented in the latter part of the OE poem. The bird symbolizes the resurrection of man; all good men, who will be saved; and Christ himself. The fire is a symbol of purification and of the final Judgment.

1 *biereð* carries
2 *in innan* to within; *trēow* tree; *torhte* bright; *frætwe* treasures
3 *wilda* wild; *fugel* bird; *wēstenne* wilderness
4 *ofer hēanne bēam* at the top of the high tree; *hūs* house; *getimbreð* builds
5 *wlitig* beautiful; *wynsum* pleasant; *gewīcað* dwells
6 *solere* sunny place; *ymbseteð* surrounds; *ūtan* on the outside
7 *lēafsceade* leafy shade; *līc* body; *feþre* plumage
8 *healfa* side (5.13); *gehwāre* every; *hālgum stencum* with holy fragrances
9 *æþelestum* finest; *blēdum* fruits
10 *Siteð* sits; *sīþes* for the journey; *fūs* ready; *Þonne* When; *swegles gim* the sky's gem
11 *sumeres* summer's; *tīd* time; *sunne* sun; *hātost* most hotly
12 *sceadu* shadow; *scīneð* shines; *gesceapu* destiny; *drēogeð* fulfils
13 *geondwlīteð* scans; *þonne* then (5.28)
14 *onhǣted* heated; *hādor* radiant
15 *Wyrta* Plants; *wearmiað* grow warm; *willsele* pleasant dwelling; *stȳmeð* steams
16 *swētum swæccum* with sweet odours; *swole* heat; *byrneð* burns
17 *feng* grasp; *neste* nest
18 *Bǣl* Fire; *onǣled* kindled; *brond* fire; *þeceð* covers
19 *heoredrēorges* of the death-sad [one]; *hrēoh* fierce [fire]; *ōnetteð* hastens
20 *fealo* yellow; *līg* flame; *feormað* devours
21 *fyrngēarum* with past years; *frōd* wise; *þigeð* eats
22 *lǣnne* transitory; *līchoman* body
23 *fǣges* of the doomed [one]; *feorhhord* life-hoard, i.e. spirit; *flǣsc* flesh; *bān* bone
24 *ādlēg* pyre-flame; *ǣleð* burns; *him* to it
25 *fyrstmearce* space of time; *ednīwe* renewed
26 *siþþan* when; *yslan* the ashes
27 *līgþræce* fire-violence; *lūcan* join; *tōgædre* together
28 *geclungne* shrunk; *tō clēowenne* to a ball; *clǣne* entirely
29 *beorhtast* brightest; *bǣle* see 18; *forgrunden* destroyed
30 *heaþorōfes* of the brave [one]; *hof* dwelling; *Hrā* corpse; *ācōlad* cooled down
31 *bānfæt* bone-vessel, i.e. body; *gebrocen* destroyed; *bryne* fire; *sweþrað* ceases
32 *of* from; *ād* see 24; *æples* of an apple; *gelīcnes* likeness
33 *ascan* ash; *gemēted* found
34 *weaxeð* grows; *wyrm* worm; *wundrum* wonderfully (5.14); *fǣger* beautiful
35 *swylce* as if; *of ǣgerum* from an egg (lit. pl.); *ūt* out; *ālǣde* were emerging (5.27)
36 *scīr* bright; *of scylle* from the shell

---

[1] *hālgum stencum* Scented spices were used in baptism. In the poem they are equated with man's good deeds, which help him to achieve eternal life.

[2] *swegles gim* The sun was commonly a symbol for Christ, who will receive the purified souls after the Day of Judgment.

[3] *neste* The nest, like the perfumes of 8 and the plants of 15, stands for good deeds in this world.

[4] *wyrm* Lactantius describes a milk-white worm which grows into an egg, from which the phoenix is reborn. The worm is also mentioned in Pliny's *Natural History* and elsewhere.

4·5 The Search for Grendel's Mother

Ic þæt londbūend,   lēode mīne,
selerǣdende   secgan hȳrde,
þæt hīe gesāwon   swylce twēgen
micle mearcstapan   mōras healdan,
ellorgǣstas.   Ðǣra ōðer wæs,   5
þæs þe hīe gewislīcost   gewitan meahton,
idese onlīcnes;   ōðer earmsceapen
on weres wæstmum   wræclāstas træd,
næfne hē wæs māra   þonne ǣnig man ōðer;
þone on geārdagum   Grendel nemdon   10
foldbūende;   nō hīe fæder cunnon,[1]
hwæþer him ǣnig wæs   ǣr ācenned
dyrnra gāsta.   Hīe dȳgel lond
warigeað wulfhleoþu,   windige næssas,
frēcne fengelād,   ðǣr fyrgenstrēam   15
under næssa genipu   niþer gewīteð,
flōd under foldan.   Nis þæt feor heonon
mīlgemearces,   þæt se mere standeð;
ofer þǣm hongiað   hrinde bearwas,
wudu wyrtum fæst   wæter oferhelmað.[2]   20
Þǣr mæg nihta gehwǣm   nīðwundor sēon,
fȳr on flōde.[3]   Nō þæs frōd leofað
gumena bearna,   þæt þone grund wite.
Ðēah þe hǣðstapa   hundum geswenced,
heorot hornum trum   holtwudu sēce,   25
feorran geflȳmed,   ǣr hē feorh seleð,
aldor on ōfre,   ǣr hē in wille,
hafelan beorgan.   Nis þæt hēoru stōw!
Þonon ȳðgeblond   up āstīgeð
won tō wolcnum,   þonne wind styreþ   30
lāð gewidru,   oð þæt lyft drysmaþ,
roderas rēotað.   Nū is se rǣd gelang
eft æt þē ānum.   Eard gīt ne const,
frēcne stōwe,   ðǣr þū findan miht

Beowulf, a poem of 3182 lines, probably dates from the eighth century; it survives in the codex known as 'Cotton Vitellius A XV' in the British Museum; see 1.5. The story concerns Danish and Swedish heroes of c. AD 500. Beowulf comes from Gotland (S. Sweden) to the help of the Danish king, Hroðgar, to slay a manlike monster called Grendel. Our extract (ll. 1345–1417) follows an episode in which Grendel's mother has killed one of Hroðgar's men in revenge for the death of her son. After line 1417, the poem continues with an account of Beowulf's single-handed victory over this second creature.

1 *þæt* correlates with *þæt* in 3 (5.28); *londbūend* land-dwellers; *lēode mīne* my people
2 *selerǣdende* hall-counsellors; *hȳrde* have heard (5.25)
3 *swylce twēgen* two such
4 *mearcstapan* walkers in the border-country; *mōras* moors; *healdan* guard (5.24)
5 *ellorgǣstas* alien spirits; *Ðǣra ōðer* One of them (5.13)
6 *þæs þe* as far as (5.10); *gewislīcost* most definitely; *gewitan* ascertain
7 *idese* of a woman; *onlīcnes* likeness; *earmsceapen* wretched
8 *on wæstmum* in the form (lit. pl.); *weres* of a man; *wræclāstas* exile-paths; *træd* trod
9 *næfne* except [that]; *māra* bigger
10 *þone* that one (5.31); *on geārdagum* in days of yore; *nemdon* called
11 *foldbūende* earth-dwellers; *nō* . . . they (i.e. the earth-dwellers) knew nothing of a father
12 *hwæþer* whether; *him* to him (i.e. to the father); *wæs ǣr ācenned* had been born (5.25)
13 *dyrnra gāsta* mysterious spirits; *dȳgel* secret; *lond* land
14 *warigeað* inhabit; *wulfhleoþu* wolf-[haunted] slopes; *windige* windy; *næssas* headlands
15 *frēcne* dangerous; *fengelād* fen-paths; *fyrgenstrēam* mountain stream
16 *genipu* mists; *niþer* down; *gewīteð* goes
17 *flōd* flood; *feor* far; *heonon* hence
18 *mīlgemearces* in mile-measure (5.13); *mere* lake
19 *hongiað* hang; *hrinde* frosty; *bearwas* woods
20 *wudu* forest; *wyrtum fæst* firm in roots, 'firm-rooted'; *wæter* water; *oferhelmað* overhangs
21 *nihta gehwǣm* every night (5.12,13); *nīðwundor* a terrifying marvel
22 *þæs* to such a degree (5.10); *frōd* experienced; *leofað* lives
23 *gumena* of men; *grund* bottom
24 *hǣðstapa* heath-walker; *hundum* by hounds; *geswenced* harassed
25 *heorot* hart; *hornum* horns (5.14); *trum* strong; *holtwudu* forest
26 *feorran* from afar; *geflȳmed* put to flight; *ǣr* sooner – correlates with *ǣr* 27 (5.28); *seleð* will give up (5.24)
27 *aldor* life; *ōfre* bank
28 *hafelan* head; *beorgan* protect; *hēoru* pleasant; *stōw* place
29 *Þonon* Thence; *ȳðgeblond* wave-turmoil; *āstīgeð* rises
30 *won* dark; *tō wolcnum* to the clouds; *styreþ* stirs up
31 *lāð* dreadful; *gewidru* storms; *lyft* air; *drysmaþ* darkens
32 *roderas* skies; *rēotað* weep; *rǣd* guidance; *gelang* dependent
33 *ānum* alone; *Eard* land; *æt* on; *gīt* . . . you do not yet know
34 *frēcne* see 15

---

[1] *nō hīe fæder cunnon* Earlier in the poem, Grendel is said to be descended from Cain, the progenitor of all evil creatures.

[2] Compare these lines, and lines 64–73 below, with the Vision of St Paul (3.4.16–26), which contains a number of features common to early accounts of the Christian hell – waste land, cold, darkness, mists, depths, and monsters. Virgil (*Aeneid* VI) similarly describes the underworld as a place of black forests, caves, and dark water.

[3] *fȳr on flōde* Possibly this means the will-o'-the-wisp; but a burning lake or river features in many Christian and other descriptions of hell.

sinnigne secg; sēc gif þū dyrre! 35
Ic þē þā fǣhðe fēo lēanige,
ealdgestrēonum, swā ic ǣr dyde,
wundnum golde, gyf þū on weg cymest.'
Bēowulf maþelode, bearn Ecgþēowes:
'Ne sorga, snotor guma! Sēlre bið ǣghwǣm, 40
þæt hē his frēond wrece, þonne hē fela murne.
Ūre ǣghwylc sceal ende gebīdan
worolde līfes; wyrce sē þe mōte
dōmes ǣr dēaþe; þæt bið drihtguman
unlifgendum æfter sēlest.[4] 45
Ārīs, rīces weard, uton hraþe fēran,
Grendles māgan gang scēawigan.
Ic hit þē gehāte: nō hē[5] on helm losaþ,
nē on foldan fæþm, nē on fyrgenholt,
nē on gyfenes grund, gā þǣr hē wille! 50
Ðȳs dōgor þū geþyld hafa
wēana gehwylces, swā ic þē wēne tō.'
Āhlēop ðā se gomela, Gode þancode,
mihtigan Drihtne, þæs se man gespræc.
Þā wæs Hrōðgāre hors gebǣted, 55
wicg wundenfeax. Wīsa fengel
geatolīc gende; gumfēþa stōp
lindhæbbendra. Lāstas wǣron
æfter waldswaþum wīde gesȳne,
gang ofer grundas, swā gegnum fōr 60
ofer myrcan mōr, magoþegna bær
þone sēlestan sāwollēasne
þāra þe mid Hrōðgāre hām eahtode.
Oferēode þā æþelinga bearn
stēap stānhliðo, stīge nearwe, 65
enge ānpaðas, uncūð gelād,
neowle næssas,[6] nicorhūsa fela;
hē fēara sum beforan gengde
wīsra monna wong scēawian,
oþ þæt hē fǣringa fyrgenbēamas 70
ofer hārne stān hleonian funde,
wynlēasne wudu; wæter under stōd
drēorig ond gedrēfed.

---

[4] See 4.6.70ff., where stoicism in the face of inevitable death, and the unflinching pursuit of fame as the best kind of memorial in a transient world, are advocated in similar terms. In the *Aeneid* X, Jupiter makes a strikingly similar speech during the battle between the Trojans and the Rutulians.

35 *sinnigne* sinful; *secg* man (see footnote 5); *sēc* . . . seek if you dare!
36 *þā fǣhðe* for that vengeance; *fēo* riches; *lēanige* will reward (5.24)
37 *ealdgestrēonum* with ancient treasures
38 *wundnum golde* with twisted gold, i.e. gold made into arm-rings; *on weg* away
39 *maþelode* spoke
40 *Ne sorga* Do not sorrow; *snotor guma* wise man; *Sēlre* . . . It is better for everyone
41 *frēond* friend; *wrece* avenge; *þonne* . . . than that he should greatly mourn
42 *Ūre ǣghwylc* Each of us; *ende* end; *gebīdan* await
43 *wyrce sē* let him strive for; *þe mōte* who is able to
44 *dōmes* glory (5.23); *dēaþe* death; *drihtguman* for a noble [-minded] man
45 *unlifgendum* lifeless; *æfter* afterwards; *sēlest* best
46 *Ārīs* Rise up; *rīces* kingdom's; *weard* guardian; *uton* let us; *hraþe* quickly
47 *māgan* kinswoman; *gang* track; *scēawigan* examine
48 *hē* see footnote 5; *on helm* under cover; *nō losaþ* will not escape (5.24,29)
49 *fæþm* bosom; *fyrgenholt* mountain forest
50 *gyfenes* of the sea; *grund* see 23; *gā* go
51 *dōgor* day; *geþyld* patience; *hafa* have
52 *wēana gehwylces* in every woe; *swā* . . . as I expect of you
53 *Āhlēop* leapt up (5.36); *se gomela* the old [man]; *þancode* thanked
54 *mihtigan Drihtne* mighty Lord; *þæs* . . . for what (5.23); *gespræc* had said (5.25)
55 *Hrōðgāre* for Hroðgar; *gebǣted* bridled
56 *wicg* steed; *wundenfeax* curly-maned; *Wīsa* wise; *fengel* lord
57 *geatolīc* splendid; *gende* = *gengde* rode; *gumfēþa* foot-troop; *stōp* stepped
58 *lindhæbbendra* of shield-bearers; *Lāstas* tracks
59 *æfter waldswaþum* along the forest paths; *wīde gesȳne* widely seen
60 *gang* see 47; *grundas* see 23; *swā* as; *gegnum* forward; *fōr* [she] had gone (5.25)
61 *myrcan* dark; *magoþegna* of the retainers; *bær* carried
62 *sēlestan* best; *sāwollēasne* soul-less, 'lifeless'
63 *hām* home; *eahtode* had guarded (5.25)
64 *Oferēode* went over; *æþelinga bearn* the son of princes, i.e. Hroðgar
65 *stēap* steep; *stānhliðo* stony slopes; *stīge* path; *nearwe* narrow
66 *enge* narrow; *ānpaðas* single-tracks; *uncūð* unknown; *gelād* see 15
67 *neowle* precipitous; *næssas* see 14; *nicorhūsa* lairs of water-monsters
68 *sum fēara wīsra monna* one of (i.e. with) a few wise men; *beforan* before
69 *wong* terrain; *scēawian* see 47
70 *fǣringa* suddenly; *fyrgenbēamas* mountain trees
71 *hārne stān* grey stone; *hleonian* lean (5.24); *funde* found (5.27)
72 *wynlēasne* joyless; *wæter* see 20
73 *drēorig* bloody; *gedrēfed* troubled

---

[5] *hē* Here and elsewhere (e.g. 50), Grendel's mother is referred to as masculine.
[6] The narrow paths and high crags of this landscape suggest another Virgilian comparison: the terrain in which Turnus prepares an ambush for Aeneas (*Aeneid* XI).

4.6 The Seafarer

Mæg ic be mē sylfum   sōðgied wrecan,
sīþas secgan,   hū ic geswincdagum
earfoðhwīle   oft þrōwade,
bitre brēostceare   gebiden hæbbe,
gecunnad in cēole   cearselda fela,   5
atol ȳþa gewealc.   Þǣr mec oft bigeat
nearo nihtwaco   æt nacan stefnan,
þonne hē be clifum cnossað.   Calde geþrungen
wǣron fēt mīne,   forste gebunden,
caldum clommum,   þǣr þā ceare seofedun   10
hāte ymb heortan.   Hungor innan slāt
merewērges mōd.   Þæt se mon ne wāt,
þe him on foldan   fǣgrost limpeð,
hū ic earmcearig   īscealdne sǣ
winter wunade   wræccan lāstum,   15
winemǣgum bidroren,
bihongen hrīmgicelum.   Hægl scūrum flēag.
Þǣr ic ne gehȳrde   būtan hlimman sǣ,
īscaldne wǣg.   Hwīlum ylfete song
dyde ic mē tō gomene,   ganetes hlēoþor   20
and huilpan swēg   fore hleahtor wera,
mǣw singende   fore medodrince.
Stormas þǣr stānclifu bēotan,   þǣr him stearn oncwæð
īsigfeþera;   ful oft þæt earn bigeal
ūrigfeþra.   Nǣnig hlēomǣga   25
fēasceaftig ferð   frēfran meahte.
Forþon him gelȳfeð lȳt   sē þe āh līfes wyn
gebiden in burgum,   bealosīþa hwōn,
wlonc and wīngāl,   hū ic wērig oft
in brimlāde   bīdan sceolde.   30
Nāp nihtscūa,   norþan snīwde,
hrīm hrūsan bond,   hægl fēol on eorþan,
corna caldast.   Forþon cnyssað nū
heortan geþōhtas,   þæt ic hēan strēamas,
sealtȳþa gelāc   sylf cunnige.   35
Monað mōdes lust   mǣla gehwylce
ferð tō fēran,   þæt ic feor heonan
elþēodigra   eard gesēce,[1]

The Seafarer is one of several short poems in the Exeter Book, concerned with the contrast of past and present, and with the mutability of life. We have omitted the last 16 lines, which are difficult to interpret, but which are essentially a continuation of the final religious statement beginning at line 103.

1 *Mæg ic* I can; *be* about; *sōðgied* true poem; *wrecan* recite
2 *sīþas* experiences; *secgan* relate; *geswincdagum* laborious days (5.23)
3 *earfoðhwīle* hardship-period; *þrōwade* suffered
4 *bitre* bitter; *brēostceare* breast-sorrow; *gebiden* experienced
5 *gecunnad* explored; *cēole* boat; *cearselda* sorrow-abodes
6 *atol* terrible; *ȳþa* waves; *gewealc* surge; *mec bigeat* occupied me
7 *nearo* anxious; *nihtwaco* night-watch; *nacan* of the boat; *stefnan* prow
8 *þonne* . . . when it tosses by the cliffs; *Calde* by cold; *geþrungen* pinched
9 *forste* by frost
10 *clommum* fetters; *seofedun* = *seofedon* sighed
11 *hāte* hot – prob. modifies *ceare*; *Hungor* Hunger; *innan* from within; *slāt* tore
12 *merewērges* of the sea-weary [one]
13 *þe him* to whom (5.10); *fǣgrost* most happily; *limpeð* it happens (5.22)
14 *earmcearig* wretched; *īscealdne* ice-cold; *sǣ* sea
15 *winter* for the winter (5.12); *wunade* remained; *wræccan* of an exile; *lāstum* in the paths
16 *winemǣgum* . . . deprived of dear kinsmen
17 *bihongen* hung about; *hrīmgicelum* with icicles; *Hægl* Hail; *scūrum* in showers; *flēag* flew
18 *būtan* except; *hlimman* resound (5.24)
19 *wǣg* wave; *ylfete* of the swan
20 *dyde* . . . I took as entertainment for myself; *ganetes* gannet; *hlēoþor* cry
21 *huilþan* of the curlew; *swēg* sound; *fore* instead of; *hleahtor* laughter; *wera* of men
22 *mǣw* seagull; *singende* singing; *medodrince* mead-drink
23 *Stormas* Storms; *stānclifu* stone cliffs; *bēotan* = *bēoton* beat; *þǣr* . . . there the tern answered them
24 *īsigfeþera* the icy-feathered [one]; *þæt earn* the eagle; *bigeal* screamed
25 *ūrigfeþra* the dewy-feathered [one]; *Nǣnig* None; *hlēomǣga* protecting kinsmen
26 *fēasceaftig* desolate; *ferð* spirit; *frēfran* comfort
27 *Forþon* Indeed; *him gelȳfeð* believes (5.23); *lȳt* little; *sē* . . . he who has the joy of life
28 *gebiden* see 4; *burgum* dwellings; *bealosīþa hwōn* few hardships (5.13)
29 *wlonc* proud; *wīngāl* wine-merry; *wērig* weary
30 *brimlāde* ocean-path; *bīdan* remain
31 *Nāp* darkened; *nihtscūa* night-shadow; *norþan* . . . it snowed from the north
32 *hrīm* frost; *hrūsan* earth; *bond* bound
33 *corna* of grains; *caldast* coldest; *Forþon* Thus; *cnyssað* . . . *þæt* thoughts buffet the heart now that . . .
34 *ic sylf* I myself; *hēan strēamas* deep seas
35 *sealtȳþa* of the salt waves; *gelāc* tumult; *cunnige* see 5
36 *Monað* urges; *lust* desire; *mǣla gehwylce* 'all the time' (5.13)
37 *ferð* spirit; *heonan* hence
38 *elþēodigra* of aliens; *eard* land; *gesēce* seek

---

[1] *elþēodigra eard* Lines 34–5 seem to indicate that the narrator is now contemplating a voyage different in kind from those he has previously mentioned – which have not taken him far from the shore, cf. 6–8. There are records of men going on dangerous voyages into exile for the sake of their spiritual welfare, but the term 'alien' (*peregrinus*) was used of good Christians, who, belonging to the City of God, are exiles in this world. *Eard* could therefore signify 'Heaven', the voyage being death, or death following a virtuous life. Lines 39–43, which suggest that the narrator has in mind the trials of every man, perhaps support this latter interpretation.

forþon nis þæs mōdwlonc mon ofer eorþan,
nē his gifena þæs gōd, nē in geoguþe tō þæs hwæt, 40
nē in his dǣdum tō þæs dēor, nē him his dryhten tō þæs hold,
þæt hē ā his sǣfōre sorge næbbe,
tō hwon hine Dryhten gedōn wille.[2]
Ne biþ him tō hearpan hyge, nē tō hringþege,
nē tō wīfe wyn, nē tō worulde hyht, 45
nē ymbe ōwiht elles, nefne ymb ȳða gewealc;
ac ā hafað longunge sē þe on lagu fundað.
Bearwas blōstmum nimað, byrig fǣgriað,
wongas wlitigiað, woruld ōnetteð;[3]
ealle þā gemoniað mōdes fūsne, 50
sefan tō sīþe, þām þe swā þenceð
on flōdwegas feor gewītan.
Swylce gēac monað geōmran reorde,
singeð sumeres weard, sorge bēodeð
bittre in brēosthord. Þæt se beorn ne wāt, 55
sēftēadig secg, hwæt þā sume drēogað,
þe þā wræclāstas wīdost lecgað.
Forþon nū mīn hyge hweorfeð ofer hreþerlocan.
Mīn mōdsefa mid mereflōde
ofer hwæles ēþel hweorfeð wīde, 60
eorþan scēatas. Cymeð eft tō mē
gīfre and grǣdig. Gielleð ānfloga,[4]
hweteð on hwælweg hreþer unwearnum
ofer holma gelagu. Forþon mē hātran sind
Dryhtnes drēamas þonne þis dēade līf, 65
lǣne on londe. Ic gelȳfe nō
þæt him eorðwelan ēce stondað.
Simle þrēora sum þinga gehwylce
ǣr his tīddæge[5] tō twēon weorþeð:
ādl oþþe yldo oþþe ecghete 70
fǣgum fromweardum feorh oðþringeð.
Forþon þæt bið eorla gehwām æftercweþendra
lof lifgendra lāstworda betst,
þæt hē gewyrce, ǣr hē on weg scyle,
fremum on foldan wið fēonda nīþ, 75
dēorum dǣdum dēofle tōgēanes,
þæt hine ælda bearn æfter hergen,

---

[2] This reminder of Judgment shows that the poet was familiar with the homiletic writings of his time: cf. footnotes 3, 6, 7.

[3] A number of sermons refer to the world hastening towards its end (and cf. 3.3, footnotes 2 and 3). Ælfric connects growth and fertility with the end of the world: '[This world] grows that it may fall' (Catholic Homilies, XL).

[4] *ānfloga* This is sometimes taken to mean the cuckoo of 62, but it may well be

39 *forþon* because; *þæs mōdwlonc* so proud
40 *nē* . . . nor so generous of his gifts; *geoguþe* youth; *tō þæs hwæt* so vigorous
41 *dǣdum* deeds; *dēor* brave; *nē* . . . nor is his lord so devoted (*hold*) to him
42 *ā* always; *his sǣfōre* concerning his sea-voyage; *sorge* anxiety
43 *tō* . . . as to what [fate] the Lord will bring him (*hine*) to
44 *Ne* . . . His mind is not on the harp; *hringþege* ring-receiving
45 *wīfe* woman; *hyht* joy
46 *ōwiht elles* anything else; *nefne* except; *gewealc* see 6
47 *longunge* longing; *sē* . . . he who sets out on the sea
48 *Bearwas* Woods; *blostmum* blossoms; *nimað* take on; *byrig fǣgriað* the dwellings grow fair
49 *wongas wlitigiað* the meadows grow beautiful; *ōnetteð* hastens on
50 *þā* those [things]; *gemoniað* remind; *mōdes fūsne* [the man] eager of spirit
51 *sefan* the heart; *tō sīþe* to the journey; *þām þe* in him who
52 *flōdwegas* ocean-paths
53 *Swylce* Likewise; *gēac* cuckoo; *geōmran reorde* with sad voice
54 *singeð* see 22; *sumeres* summer's; *weard* guardian; *bēodeð* forebodes
55 *bittre* see 4; *brēosthord* breast-hoard, i.e. the feelings of the heart
56 *sēftēadig* comfort-blessed; *secg* man; *hwæt* . . . what those few suffer
57 *þā wræclāstas lecgað* lay the exile-paths, 'travel as exiles'; *wīdost* very widely
58 *Forþon* 'For all that'; *hweorfeð* turns; *ofer* beyond; *hreþerlocan* heart-enclosure
59 *mōdsefa* mind; *mid mereflōde* along with the ocean
60 *hwæles ēþel* the whale's homeland; *wīde* widely
61 *scēatas* [over] the regions
62 *gīfre* eager; *grǣdig* hungry; *Gielleð* cries; *ānfloga* the lone flier
63 *hweteð* urges; *unwearnum* irresistibly
64 *holma* of the seas; *gelagu* the expanses; *Forþon* Thus; *drēamas* joys; *hātran* hotter 'dearer'
65 *dēade* dead
66 *lǣne* transitory; *londe* land; *gelȳfe* believe; *nō* not at all
67 *him* 'for anyone'; *eorðwelan* earthly riches; *ēce* for ever
68 *Simle* Always; *þrēora sum* one of three [things] (5.13); *þinga gehwylce* in every circumstance
69 *tīddæge* last day; *tō twēon weorþeð* comes into question
70 *ādl* disease; *yldo* age; *ecghete* sword-hatred
71 *fǣgum* from the doomed [one]; *fromweardum* 'departing'; *oðþringeð* matches
72 *Forþon* So; *þæt* anticipates *þæt* 74; *eorla gehwām* for every man; *æftercweþendra* . . . the praise (*lof*) of those living and speaking afterwards
73 *lāstworda betst* the best of trace-words, i.e. epitaphs
74 *gewyrce* may earn; *on weg* away; *scyle* must [go] (5.20)
75 *fremum* by good deeds; *wið* against; *nīþ* malice
76 *dēorum* see 41; *dēofle* the devil; *tōgēanes* against
77 *þæt* so that; *ælda* of men; *bearn* sons; *hergen* may praise (5.27)

---

a reference to the *hyge* of 58. Pliny, in his *Natural History*, and later writers such as St Augustine and Alcuin write of the ability of the soul to travel outside the body; and the notion of the free-ranging spirit – sometimes in the shape of a bird – is found in Icelandic sagas and in Irish legends.

[5] *tīddæge* The interpretation depends on an emendation; the manuscript reads *tide ge*.

and his lof siððan lifge mid englum
āwa tō ealdre, ēcan līfes blǣd,
drēam mid dugeþum.[6] Dagas sind gewitene, 80
ealle onmēdlan eorþan rīces.
Nearon nū cyningas nē cāseras
nē goldgiefan, swylce iū wǣron,
þonne hī mǣst mid him mǣrþa gefremedon
and on dryhtlicestum dōme lifdon. 85
Gedroren is þēos duguð eal, drēamas sind gewitene;
wuniað þā wācran and þās woruld healdaþ,
brūcað þurh bisgo. Blǣd is gehnǣged;
eorþan indryhto ealdað and sēarað
swā nū monna gehwylc geond middangeard: 90
yldo him on fareð, onsȳn blācað,
gomelfeax gnornað, wāt his iūwine,
æþelinga bearn eorþan forgiefene.
Ne mæg him þonne se flǣschoma, þonne him þæt feorg losað,
nē swēte forswelgan nē sār gefēlan 95
nē hond onhrēran nē mid hyge þencan.[7]
Þēah þe græf wille golde strēgan
brōþor his geborenum, byrgan be dēadum
māþmum mislicum, þæt hine mid nille.
Ne mæg þǣre sāwle, þe biþ synna ful, 100
gold tō gēoce for Godes egsan,
þonne hē hit ǣr hȳdeð þenden hē hēr leofað.[8]
Micel biþ se Meotudes egsa, forþon hī sēo molde oncyrreð;
sē gestaþelade stīþe grundas,
eorþan scēatas and uprodor. 105
Dol biþ sē þe him his Dryhten ne ondrǣdeþ: cymeð him se dēað unþinged.
Ēadig bið sē þe ēaþmōd leofaþ: cymeð him sēo ār of heofonum.
Meotod him þæt mōd gestaþelað, forþon hē in his meahte gelȳfeð.

---

[6] See 4.5.40–45 (and footnote 4) for a similar statement, but without explicit Christian overtones.

[7] These lines (88–96) suggest another comparison with Ælfric. In the homily mentioned in footnote 3, he goes on to say, 'This world is like an old man . . . in old age the man's stature is bowed, . . . his face wrinkled, . . . his breast

78 *lof* glory; *lifge* may live
79 *āwa tō ealdre* 'for ever and ever'; *ēcan* eternal; *blǣd* glory
80 *dugeþum* the valiant [in heaven]; *Dagas* days
81 *onmēdlan* splendours
82 *Nearon* There are not (5.21); *cāseras* emperors
83 *goldgiefan* gold-givers; *swylce* such as; *iū* formerly
84 *þonne . . .* when they performed (*gefremedon*) the greatest of glorious deeds (*mǣrþa*) among themselves
85 *dryhtlicestum* noblest; *dōme* renown
86 *Gedroren* declined; *duguð* valiant company
87 *wuniað* see 15; *þā wācran* the weaker [ones]
88 *brūcað* live; *bisgo* trouble; *gehnǣged* humbled
89 *indryhto* the nobility; *ealdað* grows old; *sēarað* fades
90 *geond* throughout; *middangeard* world (see 3.4, footnote 4)
91 *him on fareð* comes on him; *onsȳn* face; *blācað* grows pale
92 *gomelfeax* the grey-haired [one]; *gnornað* laments; *iūwine* former friends
93 *æþelinga* of princes; *forgiefene* [to have] given up
94 *Ne . . .* The body (*se flǣschoma*) will not then be able, when life (*þæt feorg*) fails for him
95 *swēte* sweet [things]; *forswelgan* to swallow; *sār* pain; *gefēlan* feel
96 *onhrēran* move
97 *Þēah þe . . .* Although a brother wishes to strew (*strēgan*) the grave of his brother (*geborenum*)
98 *byrgan . . .* bury [him] beside the dead
99 *māþmum mislicum* with various treasures; *þæt* i.e. such wealth; *nille* will not [go] (5.20)
100 *Ne mæg gold tō gēoce* Gold cannot [act] as a help; *þǣre sāwle* to the soul; *synna* of sins
101 *for* in the face of; *egsan* fear
102 *hȳdeð* hides; *þenden* while
103 *Meotudes* of God; *forþon . . .* because of which the earth changes itself, i.e. is changed
104 *sē* i.e. God; *gestaþelade* established; *stīþe . . .* firm foundations
105 *scēatas* see 61; *uprodor* sky
106 *Dol* Foolish; *him ondrǣdeþ* fears (5.23); *dēað* death; *unþinged* unexpected
107 *Ēadig* Blessed; *ēaþmōd* humble; *ār* grace
108 *meahte* power; *mōd* state of mind; *gelȳfeð* see 66

---

is tormented with sighs, and between his words his breath fails . . . So it is with this world.'

[8] These lines (97–102) contain echoes of Psalm 49 (48 in the Vulgate), and there is a close parallel to them in an OE homily (MS Hatton 116, p. 390).

4·7 The Wanderer

'Oft him ānhaga āre gebīdeð,
Metudes miltse, þēah þe hē mōdcearig
geond lagulāde longe sceolde
hrēran mid hondum hrīmcealde sǣ,
wadan wræclāstas: wyrd bið ful ārǣd.' 5
Swā cwæð eardstapa earfeþa gemyndig,
wrāþra wælsleahta, winemǣga hryre:
'Oft ic sceolde āna ūhtna gehwylce
mīne ceare cwīþan. Nis nū cwicra nān,
þe ic him mōdsefan mīnne durre 10
sweotule āsecgan. Ic tō sōþe wāt
þæt biþ in eorle indryhten þēaw,
þæt hē his ferðlocan fæste binde,
healde his hordcofan, hycge swā hē wille.[1]
Ne mæg wērig mōd wyrde wiðstondan, 15
nē se hrēo hyge helpe gefremman.
Forðon dōmgeorne drēorigne oft
in hyra brēostcofan bindað fæste.
Swā ic mōdsefan mīnne sceolde,
oft earmcearig ēðle bidǣled, 20
frēomǣgum feor, feterum sǣlan,
siþþan geāra iū goldwine mīnne
hrūsan heolstre biwrāh and ic hēan þonan
wōd wintercearig ofer waþema gebind,
sōhte seledrēorig sinces bryttan, 25
hwǣr ic feor oþþe nēah findan meahte
þone þe in meoduhealle mine wisse,
oþþe mec frēondlēasne frēfran wolde,
wenian mid wynnum.[2] Wāt sē þe cunnað
hū slīþen bið sorg tō gefēran 30
þām þe him lȳt hafað lēofra geholena:
warað hine wræclāst, nales wunden gold,
ferðloca frēorig, nalæs foldan blǣd;
gemon hē selesecgas and sincþege,
hū hine on geoguðe his goldwine 35
wenede tō wiste. Wyn eal gedrēas.
Forþon wāt sē þe sceal his winedryhtnes
lēofes lārcwidum longe forþolian.
Đonne sorg and slǣp somod ætgædre

The Wanderer is of the same genre as *The Seafarer* and is also in the Exeter Book.

[1] The principle of keeping one's sorrows to oneself is Germanic and heroic, and also classical and Christian.

1 *ānhaga* the solitary [one]; *āre* grace; *gebīdeð* experiences
2 *Metudes* God's; *miltse* mercy; *mōdcearig* troubled in thought
3 *geond* throughout; *lagulāde* the sea-way; *longe* for a long time (5.36)
4 *hrēran* stir; *hrīmcealde* ice-cold; *sǣ* sea
5 *wadan* travel; *wræclāstas* exile-paths; *wyrd* destiny; *ārǣd* determined
6 *eardstapa* wanderer; *earfeþa* of hardships; *gemyndig* mindful
7 *wrāþra wælsleahta* of fierce killings; *winemǣga* . . . in the fall (*hryre*) of dear kinsmen
8 *āna* alone; *ūhtna gehwylce* every dawn
9 *ceare* sorrow; *cwīþan* bewail; *cwicra nān* no one living
10 *mōdsefan* mind; *durre* dare (5.27)
11 *sweotule* openly; *āsecgan* explain; *tō sōþe* as a fact
12 *eorle* man; *indryhten* noble; *þēaw* custom
13 *ferðlocan* spirit-enclosure; *binde* bind (5.27)
14 *healde* guard; *hordcofan* treasure-chest, i.e. heart; *hycge* . . . think as he will
15 *wērig* weary; *wiðstondan* withstand
16 *hrēo* disturbed; *hyge* mind; *helþe* help; *gefremman* bring
17 *Forðon* Therefore; *dōmgeorne* glory-desiring [ones]; *drēorigne* a sad [heart]
18 *brēostcofan* heart
20 *earmcearig* wretched; *ēðle* of a native land; *bidǣled* deprived
21 *frēomǣgum* from noble kinsmen; *feterum* with fetters; *sǣlan* bind
22 *siþþan* since; *geāra iū* long ago; *goldwine* gold-friend, i.e. lord
23 *hrūsan* of the earth; *heolstre* in the darkness; *biwrāh* [I] covered; *hēan* abject; *þonan* thence
24 *wōd* went; *wintercearig* desolate as winter; *waþema* of waves; *gebind* expanse
25 *seledrēorig* 'grieving over the hall'; *sinces* of treasure; *bryttan* giver
26 *nēah* near
27 *þone þe* one who; *meoduhealle* mead-hall; *mine wisse* might know love, 'feel love for me'
28 *frēondlēasne* friendless; *frēfran* comfort
29 *wenian* entertain; *wynnum* pleasures; *sē þe cunnað* he who experiences [it]
30 *slīþen* cruel; *sorg* sorrow; *tō gefēran* as a companion
31 *þām þe* for him who; *lȳt* few; *geholena* confidants
32 *warað* preoccupies; *nales* not at all; *wunden gold* see 4.5.38
33 *frēorig* frozen; *foldan* of the earth; *blǣd* glory
34 *gemon* remembers; *selesecgas* hall-men; *sincþege* treasure-receiving
35 *on geoguðe* in youth
36 *wenede* see 29; *tō wiste* to the feast; *gedrēas* has perished (5.25)
37 *Forþon* 'And so'; *winedryhtnes* friendly lord's
38 *lārcwidum* words of advice; *forþolian* forgo
39 *Đonne* When; *slǣp* sleep; *somod ætgædre* both together

---

[2] The close relationship of lord and retainer in the society which forms the background to this poem is well illustrated throughout *The Battle of Maldon* (4.1).

earmne ānhagan   oft gebindað, 40
þinceð him on mōde   þæt hē his mondryhten
clyppe and cysse,   and on cnēo lecge
honda and hēafod,   swā hē hwīlum ǣr
in geārdagum   giefstōles brēac.[3]
Ðonne onwæcneð eft   winelēas guma, 45
gesihð him biforan   fealwe wēgas,
baþian brimfuglas,   brǣdan feþra,
hrēosan hrīm and snāw   hægle gemenged.
Þonne bēoð þȳ hefigran   heortan benne,
sāre æfter swǣsne.   Sorg bið genīwad, 50
þonne māga gemynd   mōd geondhweorfeð,
grēteð glīwstafum,   georne geondscēawað
secga geseldan.   Swimmað eft on weg.[4]
Flēotendra ferð   nō þǣr fela bringeð
cūðra cwidegiedda.[5]   Cearo bið genīwad 55
þām þe sendan sceal   swīþe geneahhe
ofer waþema gebind   wērigne sefan.
Forþon ic geþencan ne mæg   geond þās woruld
for hwan mōdsefa   mīn ne gesweorce,
þonne ic eorla līf   eal geondþence, 60
hū hī fǣrlīce   flet ofgēafon,
mōdge maguþegnas.   Swā þes middangeard
ealra dōgra gehwām   drēoseð and fealleþ.[6]
  Forþon ne mæg weorþan wīs   wer, ǣr hē āge
wintra dǣl in woruldrīce.   Wita sceal geþyldig,[7] 65
ne sceal nō tō hātheort   nē tō hrædwyrde,
nē tō wāc wiga   nē tō wanhȳdig,
nē tō forht nē tō fægen,   nē tō feohgīfre,
nē nǣfre gielpes tō georn.   Ǣr hē geare cunne
beorn sceal gebīdan,   þonne hē bēot spriceð,[8] 70
oþ þæt, collenferð,   cunne gearwe
hwider hreþra gehygd   hweorfan wille.
Ongietan sceal glēaw hæle   hū gæstlic bið,
þonne eall þisse worulde wela   wēste stondeð,[9]
swā nū missenlīce   geond þisne middangeard 75
winde biwāune   weallas stondaþ,

---

[3] This appears to refer to a ceremonial distribution of gifts. Comparable ceremonies involving a retainer and his lord are described in Icelandic sagas.

[4] *secga geseldan* The narrator may be thinking of his kinsmen and comrades as they exist in his memory; or he may mean that he is communing with their spirits. It is likely that the *flēotendra ferð* of 54 are these memories, or spirits, though it has been suggested that they are the sea-birds of 47. See 4.6, footnote 4, for the conception of the soul or spirit as able to travel independently of the body, an idea which we perhaps have again here in 55–7.

40 *earmne* see 20; *gebindað* hold fast
41 *þinceð* . . . 'he dreams' (5.22); *mondryhten* lord
42 *clyppe* embraces (5.27); *cysse* kisses; *cnēo* knee; *lecge* lays
43 *hēafod* head
44 *in geārdagum* in days of yore; *giefstōles* gift-seat; *brēac* had joy from
45 *onwæcneð* awakens; *eft* again; *winelēas guma* friendless man
46 *gesihð* sees; *biforan* before; *fealwe* tawny; *wēgas* waves
47 *baþian* bathe (5.24); *brimfuglas* sea-birds; *brǣdan* spread; *feþra* feathers
48 *hrēosan* fall; *hrīm* frost; *snāw* snow; *hægle* with hail; *gemenged* mingled
49 *þȳ hefigran* the heavier; *heortan* of the heart; *benne* wounds
50 *sāre* painful; *æfter swǣsne* for the beloved [one]; *genīwad* renewed
51 *þonne* . . . when the mind (*mōd*) surveys the memory (*gemynd*) of kinsmen
52 *grēteð* greets; *glīwstafum* joyfully; *geondscēawað* examines
53 *secga* of men; *geseldan* the companions; *Swimmað* swim; *on weg* away
54 *Flēotendra ferð* The spirit of the floating [ones]; *nō* not at all; *bringeð* brings; *fela cūðra cwidegiedda* many familiar utterances
56 *geneahhe* often
57 see 24, 15, 10
58 *Forþon* So; *geþencan* think; *geond* see 3
59 *for hwan* why; *ne gesweorce* should not grow dark
60 *þonne* when; *geondþence* think over
61 *fǣrlīce* suddenly; *flet ofgēafon* gave up the [hall] floor, i.e. died
62 *mōdge* brave; *maguþegnas* young retainers; *middangeard* world (see 3.4, footnote 4)
63 *ealra* . . . 'on every single day' (5.13,14); *drēoseð* declines
64 *Forþon* 'And so'; *ne* . . . a man cannot become wise before he has (5.27)
65 *wintra dǣl* a quantity of winters, i.e. many years; *woruldrīce* world; *Wita* wise man; *sceal* . . . must [be] patient (5.20)
66 *tō* too; *hātheort* hot-headed; *nē* nor (5.29); *hrædwyrde* hasty of speech
67 *wāc* weak; *wiga* warrior; *wanhȳdig* foolhardy
68 *forht* timid; *fægen* pleasure-loving; *feohgīfre* wealth-greedy
69 *nǣfre* never; *gielpes* for self-assertiveness; *geare cunne* 'is fully aware'
70 *gebīdan* wait
71 *collenferð* resolute
72 *hwider* whither; *hreþra* of the heart; *gehygd* the thought; *hweorfan* turn
73 *Ongietan* understand; *glēaw* wise; *hæle* man; *gæstlic* terrible; *bið* it will be (5.24)
74 *þonne* when; *wela* prosperity; *wēste* deserted
75 *missenlīce* in various places
76 *winde* by the wind; *biwāune* blown upon; *weallas* walls

---

[5] Cf. 4.3, footnote 8, for comparable 'understatements': the sense is that the narrator's 'companions' are completely silent or – if we take them to be birds – unintelligible.
[6] See 4.6.88–96 and footnote 7 for a similar comparison of the death of men with the ending of the world.
[7] Similar lists of injunctions are to be found in a number of OE homilies.
[8] *bēot* See 4.1, footnote 14, for the connotations of this word.
[9] A reference to the end of the world; cf. 4.6 and footnote 3.

hrīme bihrorene, hryðge þā ederas.[10]
Wōriað þā wīnsalo, waldend licgað
drēame bidrorene. Duguð eal gecrong
wlonc bī wealle: sume wīg fornōm, 80
ferede in forðwege; sumne fugel oþbær
ofer hēanne holm; sumne se hāra wulf
dēaðe gedǣlde;[11] sumne drēorighlēor
in eorðscræfe eorl gehȳdde.
Ȳþde swā þisne eardgeard ælda Scyppend, 85
oþ þæt burgwara breahtma lēase,
eald enta geweorc īdlu stōdon.'
Sē þonne þisne wealsteal wīse geþōhte,
and þis deorce līf dēope geondþenceð,
frōd in ferðe, feor oft gemon 90
wælsleahta worn, and þās word ācwið:
'Hwǣr cwōm mearg, hwǣr cwōm mago? Hwǣr cwōm māþþumgyfa?
Hwǣr cwōm symbla gesetu? Hwǣr sindon seledrēamas?[12]
Ēalā beorht būne, ēalā byrnwiga,
ēalā þēodnes þrym! Hū sēo þrāg gewāt, 95
genāp under nihthelm, swā hēo nō wǣre!
Stondeð nū on lāste lēofre duguþe
weal wundrum hēah, wyrmlīcum fāh;
eorlas fornōmon æsca þrȳþe,
wǣpen wælgīfru, wyrd sēo mǣre; 100
and þās stānhleoþu stormas cnyssað,
hrīð hrēosende hrūsan bindeð,
wintres wōma, þonne won cymeð,
nīpeð nihtscūa, norþan onsendeð
hrēo hæglfare hæleþum on andan. 105
Eall is earfoðlic eorþan rīce;
onwendeð wyrda gesceaft weoruld under heofonum.
Hēr bið feoh lǣne, hēr bið frēond lǣne,
hēr bið mon lǣne, hēr bið mǣg lǣne:
eal þis eorþan gesteal īdel weorþeð.' 110
Swā cwæð snottor on mōde, gesæt him sundor æt rūne.
'Til biþ sē þe his trēowe gehealdeþ, ne sceal nǣfre his torn tō rycene
beorn of his brēostum ācȳþan, nemþe hē ǣr þā bōte cunne
eorl mid elne gefremman. Wel bið þām þe him āre sēceð,
frōfre tō Fæder on heofonum, þǣr ūs eal sēo fæstnung stondeð.' 115

---

[10] Ruins are found elsewhere in OE poetry, and also in medieval Latin, as symbols of mutability. Another Exeter Book poem, *The Ruin*, is a meditation on a derelict Roman city. The *enta* of 87 may be a reference to the Romans, and the phrase *wyrmlīcum fāh* in 98 may be descriptive of Roman bas-reliefs, which often featured snake-like creatures.

77 *bihrorene* covered; *hryðge* storm-swept; *ederas* buildings
78 *Wōriað* crumble; *wīnsalo* wine-halls; *waldend* rulers
79 *drēame* of joy; *bidrorene* deprived; *Duguð* noble company; *gecrong* has fallen (5.25)
80 *wlonc* proud; *bī* by; *sume* . . . battle took some
81 *ferede* carried; *in forðwege* on the journey hence; *sumne* . . . one a bird bore off
82 *hēanne holm* the deep sea; *hāra* grey; *wulf* wolf
83 *dēaðe* to death; *gedǣlde* handed over; *drēorighlēor eorl* sad-faced man
84 *eorðscræfe* grave; *gehȳdde* hid
85 *Ȳþde* destroyed; *eardgeard* city; *ælda* of men; *Scyppend* Creator
86 *burgwara* of the citizens; *breahtma* rejoicings; *lēase* deprived
87 *eald* old; *enta* of giants; *geweorc* works; *īdlu* empty
88 *Sē* He who; *wealsteal* walled place; *wīse* wisely; *geþōhte* has pondered
89 *deorce* dark; *dēope* deeply
90 *frōd* wise; *ferðe* see 54; *feor* far [back]; *gemon* see 34
91 *wælsleahta worn* many killings; *word* words; *ācwið* utters
92 *Hwǣr* . . . Where has the steed gone; *mago* young man; *māþþumgyfa* treasure-giver
93 *symbla* of banquets; *gesetu* dwellings; *seledrēamas* hall-joys
94 *Ēalā* Alas; *beorht* bright; *būne* cup; *byrnwiga* mailed warrior
95 *þrym* glory; *þrāg* time
96 *genāp* has darkened; *nihthelm* the cover of night; *swā* . . . as if it had never been
97 *on lāste* in the track, 'in their place'; *duguþe* see 79
98 *weal* wall; *wundrum hēah* wonderfully high; *wyrmlīcum* with serpent forms; *fāh* decorated
99 *eorlas* . . . the power (*þrȳþe*, pl.) of ash-wood [spears] has carried off the men
100 *wælgīfru* slaughter-greedy; *wyrd* . . . the glorious (*mǣre*) destiny
101 *stānhleoþu* stony slopes; *stormas* storms; *cnyssað* batter
102 *hrīð* snowstorm; *hrēosende* see 48; *hrūsan* see 23
103 *wintres* winter's; *wōma* noise; *won* dark[ness]
104 *nīpeð* grows dark; *nihtscūa* night-shadow; *norþan* from the north; *onsendeð* sends out
105 *hrēo* fierce; *hæglfare* hailstorm; *hæleþum* . . . to the vexation of men (5.14)
106 *earfoðlic* fraught with hardship; *rīce* realm
107 *onwendeð* changes; *wyrda* of destiny (lit. pl.); *gesceaft* the ordered course
108 *feoh* property; *lǣne* transitory; *frēond* friend
109 *mǣg* kinsman
110 *gesteal* establishment, i.e. the things of this world; *īdel* useless
111 *snottor* the wise [one]; *gesæt him* sat (5.23); *sundor* apart; *æt rūne* in meditation
112 *Til* Good; *trēowe* faith; *gehealdeþ* keeps; *torn* bitterness; *tō rycene* too readily
113 *of* from; *brēostum* breast (lit. pl.); *ācȳþan* reveal; *nemþe* unless; *bōte* remedy; *gefremman* achieve
114 *mid elne* with zeal; *Wel* Well; *āre* see 1
115 *frōfre* comfort; *fæstnung* stronghold

---

[11] In several OE poems, there are allusions to wolves and birds – usually the eagle and the raven – as attendant on scenes of battle; cf. 4.1.90f.

[12] It was a commonplace in Latin homilies to pose the rhetorical question, 'Where are (*Ubi sunt*) the pleasures and the heroes of the past?' This theme remained popular in European poetry; cf. Henryson's *Testament of Cresseid* and Villon's *Ballade des dames du temps jadis*. Compare *The Seafarer* (4.6.80–88), where the narrator looks back in a similar way.

4.8 Riddles

(*a*) Wiht cwōm gongan þǣr weras sǣton
monige on mæðle, mōde snottre;
hæfde ān ēage ond ēaran twā,
ond twēgen fēt, twelf hund hēafda,
hrycg ond wombe ond honda twā, 5
earmas ond eaxle, ānne swēoran
ond sīdan twā. Saga hwæt ic hātte.

(*b*) Neb wæs mīn on nearwe, ond ic neoþan wætre,
flōde underflōwen, firgenstrēamum
swīþe besuncen, ond on sunde āwōx 10
ufan ȳþum þeaht, ānum getenge
līþendum wuda līce mīne.
Hæfde feorh cwico, þā ic of fæðmum cwōm
brimes ond bēames on blacum hrægle;
sume wǣron hwīte hyrste mīne, 15
þā mec lifgende lyft upp āhōf,
wind of wǣge, siþþan wīde bær
ofer seolhbaþo. Saga hwæt ic hātte.

(*c*) Oft mec fæste bilēac frēolicu mēowle,
ides on earce, hwīlum up ātēah 20
folmum sīnum ond frēan sealde,
holdum þēodne, swā hīo hāten wæs.
Siðþan mē on hreþre hēafod sticade,
nioþan upweardne, on nearo fēgde.
Gif þæs ondfengan ellen dohte, 25
mec frætwedne fyllan sceolde
rūwes nāthwæt. Rǣd hwæt ic mǣne.

The Exeter Book contains almost a hundred Riddles, varying widely in tone and extent. No solutions are given in the original and many are by no means certain. The three selected here are (*a*) 85, (*b*) 10, and (*c*) 61, as they are commonly numbered in editions of the Exeter Book.

(*a*) The solution is probably 'one-eyed onion-man': there is a Latin riddle with this answer dating from about the fifth century AD.

1 *Wiht* creature; *cwōm gongan* came walking (5.24); *weras* men
2 *mæðle* council; *mōde* in mind; *snottre* wise
3 *ēage* eye; *ēaran* ears; *twā* two
4 *twēgen* two; *twelf hund* twelve hundred; *hēafda* heads
5 *hrycg* back; *wombe* stomach
6 *earmas* arms; *eaxle* shoulders; *ānne swēoran* one neck
7 *sīdan* sides; *Saga* Say; *hātte* am called (5.26)
8 *Neb* beak; *on nearwe* in a narrow place; *neoþan* beneath; *wætre* water
9 *flōde* by the flood; *underflōwen* underflowed, i.e. borne up; *firgenstrēamum* by mountain streams
10 *besuncen* submerged; *sunde* sea; *āwōx* [I] grew up
11 *ufan* from above; *ȳþum* waves; *þeaht* covered; *ānum līþendum wuda* to a moving [piece of] wood; *getenge* clinging
12 *līce mīne* with my body
13 *feorh* spirit; *cwico* living; *of fæðmum* from the embraces
14 *brimes* sea; *bēames* wood; *blacum* black; *hrægle* clothing
15 *hwīte* white; *hyrste* decorations
16 *lifgende* living; *lyft* air; *upp* up
17 *of wǣge* from the wave; *wīde* far
18 *seolhbaþo* seal-bath, i.e. sea
19 *bilēac* enclosed; *frēolicu* fine; *mēowle* woman
20 *ides* woman; *earce* chest; *ātēah* pulled out
21 *folmum sīnum* with her hands; *frēan* to the lord; *sealde* gave
22 *holdum* devoted; *hīo* = *hēo*; *hāten* commanded
23 *hreþre* bosom; *hēafod* see 4; *sticade* thrust
24 *nioþan* from beneath; *upweardne* upward; *on nearo* see 8; *fēgde* fixed
25 *þæs ondfengan* the receiver's; *ellen* strength; *dohte* was good
26 *mec frætwedne* me, the adorned [one]; *fyllan* fill
27 *rūwes nāthwæt* something rough; *Rǣd* Explain; *mǣne* signify

---

(*b*) There is little dispute that the solution here is 'barnacle goose', which was popularly thought to grow from the barnacles that attach themselves to ships. There is a version of the legend in ch. 26 of the fourteenth-century *Mandeville's Travels*.

(*c*) This riddle, like several others, depends for its effectiveness on a *double entendre*; of the 'innocent' meanings proposed, 'helmet' is perhaps the most convincing.

5 Outlines of the Language

The Noun Phrase

5.1 OE nouns may be masculine, neuter, or feminine, irrespective of biological sex; thus *stān* 'stone' is masculine, *wīf* 'woman' is neuter, and *fyrd* 'army' is feminine.

5.2 Nouns show inflectional distinctions for up to four cases – nominative, accusative, genitive, dative – and the pattern of case endings gives us four broad classes of nouns: the *general masculine*, the somewhat similar *general neuter*, the *general feminine*, and the *-an* class where there is little difference between the genders.

5.3 Adjectives agree with their related nouns in gender, case, and number, but in addition they have an inflectional distinction depending on whether they follow a demonstrative (when they have the *definite inflection*) or do not (when they have the *indefinite inflection*). The definite inflection is also used in vocative phrases, e.g. 3.2.18.

5.4 There are two demonstratives, *þæt* 'the, that', and *þis* 'this'. Both are inflected for gender, case, and number. The articles of ModE are often totally absent: *wīcinga ār* '*a* messenger of *the* Vikings'.

5.5 In the following table, we combine the illustration of the three *general* (G) noun classes with the *indefinite* adjective inflection and the *definite* adjective inflection, the latter accompanied by the *þæt* demonstrative:

General masculine nouns, 'good king':

sing	*nom*	*indef*	gōd[1]	cyning
		def	se gōda	
	acc	*indef*	gōdne	cyning
		def	þone gōdan	
	gen	*indef*	gōdes	cyninges
		def	þæs gōdan	
	dat	*indef*	gōdum	cyninge
		def	þǣm gōdan	
plur	*nom & acc*	*indef*	gōde	cyningas
		def	þā gōdan	
	gen	*indef*	gōdra	cyninga
		def	þāra gōdena	
	dat	*ind & def*	(þǣm) gōdum	cyningum

General neuter and feminine nouns, 'wide land' *neut.*, 'strong cross' *fem.*:

sg	*na*	*indef*	wīd[1]	land
		def	þæt wīde	
	g	*indef*	wīdes	landes
		def	þæs wīdan	
	d	*indef*	wīdum	lande
		def	þǣm wīdan	
pl	*na*	*indef*	wīd[2]	land[2]
		def	þā wīdan	
	g	*indef*	wīdra	landa
		def	þāra wīdena	
	d	*ind & def*	(þǣm) wīdum	landum

sg	*n*	*indef*	strang[3]	rōd[3]
		def	sēo strange	
	a	*indef*	strange	rōde
		def	þā strangan	
	gd	*indef*	strangre	rōde
		def	þǣre strangan	
pl	*na*	*indef*	stranga	rōda
		def	þā strangan	
	g	*indef*	strangra	rōda
		def	þāra strangena	
	d	*ind & def*	(þǣm) strangum	rōdum

Notes

(1) Numerous adjectives have an *-e* ending, e.g. *rīce* 'powerful'.
(2) Where a short syllable precedes, we have *-u* endings, e.g. *trumu scipu* 'satisfactory ships'.
(3) As in (2), e.g. *gramu cwalu* 'hideous slaughter'.

5·6 The next table shows the *-an* noun class (*AN*) and the *þis* demonstrative:

		masc	*neut*	*fem*
sg	*n*	þes guma 'man'	þis ēage 'eye'	þēos byrne 'coat-of-mail'
	a	þisne guman	þis ēage	þās byrnan
	g	þisses guman	þisses ēagan	þisse byrnan
	d	þissum guman	þissum ēagan	þisse byrnan

		no gender distinction
pl	*na*	þās guman, ēagan, byrnan
	g	þissa gumena, ēagena, byrnena
	d	þissum gumum, ēagum, byrnum

5·7 There are many minor irregularities in noun inflection which we must ignore in this book, but some common nouns with major irregularities should be noted:

	sg	*pl*
na	mann (*masc* 'man')	menn
g	mannes	manna
d	menn	mannum

Similarly *fōt* 'foot', d.sg. *fēt*; *bōc* 'book' (fem., with g.sg. *bōce*); *burg* 'stronghold' (fem., with g.sg. *burge*, d.sg. *byrig*).

5·8 *Comparative and Superlative*

The comparative of adjectives is formed by adding *-ra* (always with the definite inflection: 5.6), of adverbs by adding *-or*. The superlative has the ending *-ost* (usually with the definite inflection in the case of adjectives). There are several irregular items:

	ADJECTIVE			ADVERB		
'good'	gōd	betra / sēlra	betst / sēlest	wel	bet / sēl	betst / sēlest
'long'	lang	lengra	lengest	lange	leng	lengest
'little'	lȳtel	lǣssa	lǣst	lȳt	lǣs	lǣst
'great, much'	micel	māra	mǣst	micle	mā	mǣst
'evil'	yfel	wyrsa	wyrst	yfle	wyrs	wyrst

Like *lang* in having a vowel change in the comp. and superl. are *eald* 'old', *geong* 'young', *hēah* 'high', *strang* 'strong'.

5·9 *Personal Pronouns*

There are gender differences only in the 3rd person singular.

	1ST PERSON, 'I, WE'		2ND PERSON, 'YOU'	
	sg	*pl*	*sg*	*pl*
n	ic	wē	þū	gē
a	mē, mec	ūs	þē	ēow
g	mīn	ūre	þīn	ēower
d	mē	ūs	þē	ēow

3RD PERSON, 'HE, IT, SHE, THEY'

	sg			*pl*
	masc	*neut*	*fem*	
n	hē	hit	hēo	hī
a	hine	hit	hī	hī
g	his	his	hire	hira
d	him	him	hire	him

Notes

(1) The personal pronouns are used also as reflexives: *he hine reste* 'he rested himself' (4.3.64).
(2) As well as singular and plural, the 1st and 2nd person have a dual number, meaning 'we-two', 'you-two'; e.g. *unc*, 4.3.48.
(3) Genitives such as *mīn* can take the indefinite adjective inflection (5.5).

5.10 The demonstratives *þæt* and *þis* (5.5,6) are also used pronominally both as demonstratives (*æfter þām* 'after that' 3.1.1, *sē gewāt* 'that [thing, i.e. the spear] went' 4.1.134), and as relatives (e.g. 3.2.4; 3.3.14), though the usual relative pronoun is the invariable *þe* (as in 3.3.4, 9, 12, 13, 17). When genitive or dative was required, *þe* could be accompanied by the relevant form of personal pronoun; thus *þe him* 'that to him', i.e. 'to whom' (4.7.10). From *þæt,* we have several important adverbial expressions such as *þæs* 'so much' (e.g. 4.5.22) and *þȳ* or *þē* 'by so much' (e.g. 4.1.130, 296–7); and from *þis* an 'instrumental' form *þȳs*.

Unstressed Forms

5.11 By about AD 1000, inflectional endings were often blurred in pronunciation, so that *-um, -on, -an, -en* could sound alike. As a result, numerous 'reverse' spellings are found (e.g. 3.1.5; 3.4.22; 4.1.5; 4.1.7), just as in ModE we sometimes hesitate between *-ant* and *-ent* in spelling *dependent.* Unstressed words such as determiners and pronouns varied in spelling a good deal, doubtless on similar grounds: e.g. *þone* appears as *þæne* in 3.1.7, *hira* as *heora* in 3.2.4 and elsewhere. Cf. also 2.4.

The Functions of the Cases

5.12 The *accusative* marks the direct object of most transitive verbs (but see also 5.23), and the complement of some prepositions which imply movement: *þurh ðone æþelan þegen* '(it went) through the noble thane', 4.1.135. In addition, the accusative is used in adverbial phrases expressing extent: *wē ðǣr gōde hwīle stōdon* 'we stood there for a long time', 4.3.70.

5.13 In addition to the various uses of the *genitive* that remain in Modern English, there were additional ones in OE. In particular, (*a*) a descriptive use as in *ic wæs miccles cynnes* 'I was of great lineage', 4.1.201, *wīges heard* 'fierce in battle'; (*b*) a partitive use as in *ūre sum* 'one of us', *ǣgþer hira* 'each of them', *manna fela* 'many men' (*fela* itself is invariable); (*c*) some prepositions in certain uses (cf. 4.1.115); (*d*) adverbial uses as in *ealles* 'entirely', *āhtes* 'of any value', *ēode his weges* '(he) went on his way'. See also 5.23.

5.14 The *dative* is used for the indirect object with verbs of telling, giving, etc. (see also 5.23), and with most prepositions. In addition, there are numerous adverbial uses and special idioms; for example, *hwīlum* 'at times', *folce tō frōfre* 'as a comfort to the people', *forste gebunden* 'bound with frost', *wundum sweltan* 'die of wounds', 4.1.277, *wintrum geong* 'young in years'. The dative is used as a kind of possessive in expressions like *him æt fōtum* 'at his feet', 4.1.103 (cf. also 4.1.129, 136), and as a reflexive with verbs such as 'be' (e.g. 4.2.62).

Verbs and the Verb Phrase

5.15 Verbs show distinctions of *number*, *tense*, *mood* and (in the indicative singular) *person*. The forms are identified by a combination of base forms (e.g. *bycg-* and *boht-* with the verb 'buy') and endings such as *-e*, *-að*, *-on*. Careful study of the vertical matching in 5.17 and 5.18 will show that from a knowledge of a small number of forms for each verb, the '*principal parts*', the whole set of distinctions for each verb can be worked out. Except for the few irregular verbs to which this does not apply, the principal parts are given with each verb in the glossary.

Note Infinitives and participles are sometimes inflected; e.g. *hæbbenne*, 3.3.14.

5.16 According to the pattern of inflections, we distinguish three types of verb: *D* (those with past participles ending with *-d* or sometimes *-t*), *N* (those with past participles in *-(e)n*), and *Irregular*.

5.17 *The D verbs* constitute the vast majority. The principal parts are the *infinitive*, the *present indicative 3rd pers. sg.*, and the *past indic. 3rd pers. sg*. There are several subtypes of D verbs, as illustrated by *lufian* 'love', *fremman* 'perform', and *bycgan* 'buy':

PRESENT

(Infinitive)		*lufian*	*fremman*	*bycgan*
(Indicative 3rd sg)		*lufað*	*fremeð*	*bygð*
Indicative	*sg* (ic)	lufie	fremme	bycge
	(þū)	lufast	fremest	bygst
	(hē)	lufað	fremeð	bygð
	pl (wē, gē, hī)	lufiað	fremmað	bycgað
Subjunctive	*sg* (ic, þū, hē)	lufie	fremme	bycge
	pl (wē, gē, hī)	lufien	fremmen	bycgen
Imperative	*sg*	lufa	freme	byge
	pl	lufiað	fremmað	bycgað
Participle		lufiende	fremmende	bycgende

PAST

(Indicative 3rd sg)		*lufode*	*fremede*	*bohte*
Indicative	*sg* (ic)	lufode	fremede	bohte
	(þū)	lufodest	fremedest	bohtest
	(hē)	lufode	fremede	bohte
	pl (wē, gē, hī)	lufodon	fremedon	bohton
Subjunctive	*sg* (ic, þū, hē)	lufode	fremede	bohte
	pl (wē, gē, hī)	lufoden	fremeden	bohten
Participle		gelufod	gefremed	geboht

5.18 *The N verbs* are more complicated, though many of the endings in 5.17 occur in similar use. The principal parts are the *infinitive*, the *present indicative 3rd pers. sg.*, the *past indic. 3rd pers. sg.*, the *past indic. pl.*, and the *past participle.* There are several subtypes, as illustrated by *helpan* 'help', *cēosan* 'choose', and *sēon* 'see':

PRESENT

(Infinitive)		*helpan*	*cēosan*	*sēon*
(Indicative 3rd sg)		*helpð*	*cȳst*	*syhð*
Indicative	*sg* (ic)	helpe	cēose	sēo
	(þū)	helpst	cȳst	syhst
	(hē)	helpð[1]	cȳst[1]	syhð
	pl (wē, gē, hī)	helpað	cēosað	sēoð
Subjunctive	*sg* (ic, þū, hē)	helpe	cēose	sēo
	pl (wē, gē, hī)	helpen	cēosen	sēon
Imperative	*sg*	help	cēos	seoh
	pl	helpað	cēosað	sēoð
Participle		helpende	cēosende	sēonde

PAST

(Indicative 3rd sg)		*healp*	*cēas*	*seah*
(Indicative 3rd pl)		*hulpon*	*curon*	*sāwon*
(Participle)		*geholpen*	*gecoren*	*gesewen*
Indicative	*sg* (ic)	healp	cēas	seah
	(þū)	hulpe	cure	sāwe
	(hē)	healp	cēas	seah
	pl (wē, gē, hī)	hulpon	curon	sāwon
Subjunctive	*sg* (ic, þū, hē)	hulpe	cure	sāwe
	pl (wē, gē, hī)	hulpen	curen	sāwen
Participle		geholpen	gecoren	gesewen

Note (1) Uncontracted forms in *-eð* also occur; e.g. *gebīdeð* 'experiences', 4.7.1.

5.19 *Irregular verbs* can in some cases be reconstructed from principal parts of the D or N types, but there are major exceptions.

5.20 Some irregular verbs are mixtures, in part resembling N verbs (in their present) and D verbs (in their past). Moreover, in individual instances, some parts occur only rarely or not at all. For example, *sculan* 'be obliged to' has no participles, and its commonest forms are:

	PRESENT INDICATIVE	PAST INDICATIVE
sg (ic)	sceal	sceolde
(þū)	scealt	sceoldest
(hē)	sceal	sceolde
pl (wē, gē, hī)	sculon	sceoldon

The relevant parts of other common irregular verbs are:

	PRESENT			PAST
	(ic)	(þū)	(wē)	(hē)
cunnan 'know how to'	cann	canst	cunnon	cūðe
magan 'be able'	mæg	meaht, miht	magon	meahte, mihte
þurfan 'need'	þearf	þearft	þurfon	þorfte
— 'dare'	dearr	dearst	durron	dorste
(ge)munan 'remember'	-man	-manst	-munon	-munde
dugan 'be of use'	dēah	—	dugon	dohte
āgan 'have'	āh	āhst	āgon	āhte
— 'be allowed'	mōt	mōst	mōton	mōste
witan 'know'	wāt	wāst	witon	wiste
willan 'want'	wille	wilt	willað	wolde

Notes

(1) *Dōn* 'do' and *gān* 'go' also resemble both D and N verbs, but their inflections can be inferred from the parts given in the glossary.

(2) Present subjunctive forms occur such as *mæge*, *mote*, *wille* (e.g. 4.1.21), *dyrre* (4.5.35), *scyle* (4.6.74). But *-e* forms occur more widely, irrespective of number, tense, or mood, when preceding the pronouns *wē*, *gē* (e.g. 4.1.18, 43).

(3) With several of these auxiliary verbs, 'be' or a verb of motion can be understood without being expressed (e.g. 4.1.48, 296, 301).

5.21 The forms of the verb 'be', *bēon* and *wesan*, are exceptionally irregular:

		PRESENT		PAST
Indicative	*sg* (ic)	eom	bēo	wæs
	(þū)	eart	bist	wǣre
	(hē)	is	bið	wæs
	pl (wē, gē, hī)	sind(on)	bēoð	wǣron
Subjunctive	*sg* (ic, þū, hē)	sȳ	bēo	wǣre
	pl (wē, gē, hī)	sȳn	bēon	wǣren
Imperative	*sg*	wes	bēo	
	pl	wesað	bēoð	
Participles		wesende	bēonde	gebēon

Note Forms corresponding to modern 'are' are rare in most OE texts, but cf. 4.6.82.

5.22 *Verbs and their Subjects*

Subjects were frequently left unexpressed: e.g. *hēt* '[he] ordered', 4.1.46. With impersonal constructions, this was the norm: *mē ofhrēow* '[it] saddened me', 3.3.11; *mē þinceð* '[it] seems to me'; *ēow is gerȳmed* '[it] is cleared for you', 4.1.77. But sometimes such impersonal subjects were expressed, e.g. *hit him þūhte* 'it seemed to them', 4.1.50.

5.23 *Verbs and their Objects*

Most transitive verbs have the direct object in the accusative, and if there is an indirect object it is in the dative: *geaf gōdne hring þǣm menn* 'he gave the man a fine ring'. Some verbs however have the direct object in the dative (e.g. *derian* 'harm', *sceððan* 'injure', *beorgan* 'save', *helpan* 'help', *andswarian* 'answer') and others have it in the genitive (e.g. *gewilnian* 'desire', *wyrnan* 'withhold', *gemunan* 'remember', *wēnan* 'expect', *brūcan* 'enjoy', *bīdan* 'await', *þurfan* 'need', *wealdan* 'control', *geunnan* 'grant', *þancian* 'thank', *reccan* 'care for'). Several verbs corresponding to intransitives in ModE have reflexive objects; e.g. *wendan* 'go' (cf. 3.2.16), *gangan* 'go' (cf. 4.1.24), *licgan* 'lie' (cf. 4.1.284).

Tense, Aspect, Voice

5.24 The present tense forms were used also to express the future (e.g. 3.4.4), *willan* plus infinitive normally implying volition rather than tense, *sculan* plus infinitive implying obligation. The simple tense forms also served for the aspectual contrast represented in ModE *I work* and *I am working*, though the rare construction illustrated by *wæs gesēonde* (3.4.16) often seems to imply something like the ModE 'progressive' *be* + *-ing*. The same applies to some constructions with the infinitive, as in *cōm gangan* 'came walking' (cf. 4.8.1). In general, however, an infinitive clause has no aspectual implication: *Ic geseah hine cuman* corresponds equally to 'I saw him come' and 'I saw him coming'. Sometimes *ongan* plus infinitive was used as equivalent to the simple past rather than indicating an ingressive aspect, 'began to . . .'

5.25 Although *habban* plus past participle was sometimes used to express perfect or pluperfect (e.g. 4.1.221; 3.2.1; 4.1.273), it was quite general to leave the distinction to be implied by the context alone. For example, *nū gē becōmon* 'now that you have come', 4.1.42; *þe hī worhtan* 'which they had brought about', 3.1.5. Where pluperfect is meant, however, it was common to have the adverb *ǣr* 'before' in the clause: e.g. 4.1.142, 182.

5.26 Instead of the passive voice, we often find the indefinite pronoun *man* 'one' with the active (e.g. 3.1.3), but *wesan* or *weorðan* plus past participle could also be used, as in *wæs hāten* 'was called' (4.1.59), *wearð gewundod* 'got wounded' (4.1.119). In the case of *hātan*, there was in fact an inflectional contrast available for active and passive in the past tense: *hēt* 'he called', *hātte* 'he was called' (cf. 3.2.4).

It is convenient to regard the infinitive as being potentially passive: cf. 3.3.14; 4.1.46.

Features of the Clause

The Use of the Subjunctive

5.27 In independent clauses, the subjunctive is used as a 'third-person imperative': *gielde hē* 'let him pay, he must pay', 3.4.8. But for the most part, the subjunctive occurs in a wide variety of subordinate clauses where, in one way or another, no claim is being made as to truth-value. For example:

(*a*) Hypothetical conditions, as in 3.4.7, 10.
(*b*) Concessive clauses, as in 4.5.24–5.
(*c*) Indirect requests, as in 4.1.241.
(*d*) Indirect questions, as in 3.2.9.
(*e*) Non-factual noun clauses, as in *wēnde þæt wǣre hit ūre hlāford* 'thought that it was our lord', 4.1.224.
(*f*) Comparative clauses, as in 4.1.179.
(*g*) Clauses dependent on subjunctive-demanding clauses, as in 4.1.219.

Correlation and Subordination

5.28 A widespread way of subordinating one clause to another was to introduce matching particles into each, as in ModE '*the* more *the* merrier' or as in 4.1.297, *mōd sceal þē māre, þē ūre mægen lȳtlað* 'courage must be *the* greater *as* our strength lessens'. Compare also *wēnde þæs formoni man þæt wǣre hit ūre hlāford* 'many a man thought *that*, [namely] *that* it was our lord', 4.1.223. Note also the relation between *þæt* in 4.1.20 and *þæt* in the following line; likewise 4.1.68–9; *swilce . . . swilce*, 3.3.19f.

Correlation has the effect that the same particle can correspond to either a conjunct or a subordinator in ModE. Thus *swā* can mean 'so' and 'as', *þǣr* 'there' or 'where', *þā* 'then' or 'when', *forþon* 'because' or 'therefore' (e.g. 4.2.4–5). For example: *Ðā se cyngc þæt geseah, þā nam hē Apollonies hand* '*When* the king saw that, *then* he took A.'s hand', 3.2.15.

Negation

5.29 Clauses were made negative by placing *ne* before the auxiliary or (if there was no auxiliary) the main verb: cf. 3.2.9; 4.1.164; 4.1.80. Multiple negation was common, and *ne* could be reinforced by another negative particle which usually followed the negated auxiliary or main verb, as in *hē ne wandode nā*, lit. 'he did not hesitate not-ever', 4.1.252. Co-ordinated negation was expressed with *nē . . . nē*, as in 3.3.11; 4.5.49–50.

5.30 The particle *ne* combined with the adverbs *ǣfre* and *ā* 'ever' to give the two words meaning 'never', *nǣfre* and *nā* or *nō* (as well as the intensified form of the latter, *nāwiht* 'never at all', which was contracted to *noht* 'nought, not'). In a similar way, there are four verbs with which *ne* combined (*wesan* 'be', *habban* 'have', *willan* 'wish', *witan* 'know'), so that we have negative forms such as *nis* 'isn't', *nǣron* 'weren't', *næfde* 'hadn't', *nolde* 'didn't want', *ic nāt* 'I don't know' (3.2.12), *niste hē* 'he didn't know' (3.2.2).

Order of Sentence Elements

5.31 As well as arrangements like *Ōswald forlēt þis līf* 'O. gave up this life' (3.1.8), normal in ModE, we find considerable variety of order in OE. Indeed, the exact reverse of the type just illustrated occurs in the preceding line: *Þæne rǣd gerǣdde Siric* 'S. decided on that plan' (3.1.7), where we recognize that the writer has chosen to mention the object first, because it is already known about, but to delay revealing the subject until, in end position, it can have the greatest impact. Similarly, where the object is a pronoun (and hence obviously known about), the verb frequently takes up the climactic end-position: *ic hine wāt* 'I know him', 3.2.18.

5.32 When a clause opens with a conjunct, it is commonly followed immediately by the first (or only) part of the verb phrase. For example (with initial *swā*), 4.1.106, 264; (with *þǣr*) 4.1.170, 285. This is especially so with *ðā* 'then': *Ðā nam Apollonius þæt gewrit* 'Then A. took the letter', 3.2.13. By contrast, when a clause opens with a subordinator, the verb phrase (or its main item) is usually put in final position: *þæt ic ðās bōc of Ledenum gereorde tō Engliscre sprǣce āwende* 'that I should turn this book from the Latin language into the English speech', 3.3.7; *þā noldon æt þām forda flēam gewyrcan* 'who would not take to flight at the ford', 4.1.65. Cf. also 3.1.18; 4.1.67, 68, 69; 4.1.183, 184, 185; 4.1.256; 4.1.262, 263. Since the same item can be a conjunct or a subordinator (cf. 5.28), it is the position of the verb that provides the distinction: *þā hē byre hæfde* 'when he had the chance', 4.1.105; *þonne wē bēot āhōfon* 'when we shouted vows', 4.1.197.

Lexicology

5.33 It is obviously essential for the student to recognize that many words in OE are the 'same' as in ModE, however disguised by different pronunciation and spelling (*mann, līf, gēar, þūsend,* etc). Many of course have changed their meaning as well (*ealdorman,* for example) and many have been replaced by the words (from French, Latin and other languages) that we have adopted over the past 900 years (for *swīðe,* we now have *very,* for example).

5.34 But in addition to using his knowledge of ModE, the student should cultivate the habit of seeing regularities of relation between OE words themselves. Thus there are many nouns and adjectives with related verbs; e.g.

eard 'dwelling place'	*eardian* 'dwell'
lufu 'love'	*lufian* 'love'
beorht 'bright'	*beorhtian* 'shine'

5·35 We need to recognize also that many of the long words encountered are compounds of words that may have been met already, e.g.

sǣrima 'sea-rim', i.e. 'coast'
bōccræft 'book-craft, literacy'
gōdspell 'good story, gospel'

even though some of the compounding practices of OE were different from ours today (e.g. *brūnecg* 'bright edg*ed*', *fealohilte* 'yellow-hilt*ed*'), and many of those occurring in the poetry are of that striking kind of poetic periphrasis known as the *kenning* (cf. 1.4); e.g. *sincgifa* 'treasure-giver, lord', *feorhhūs* 'life-house, body'.

5·36 Above all, we need to note that several prefixes and suffixes recur frequently, with regular effect on the meaning of the word so modified. Some of the commonest have remained in ModE (e.g. *mis-*, *ofer-*, *un-*; *-dōm*, *-ere*, *-ful*, *-ig* as in *grǣdig* 'greedy', *-hād* '-hood', *-isc*, *-lēas* as in *winelēas* 'friendless', *-nes(s)*, *-scipe*), but in some important instances we need to know the specifically OE usage:

Prefixes

ā- gives completeness and sometimes intensification to the meaning: *āhēawan* 'cut *off*', *ārǣran* 'raise *up*', *āflȳman* 'rout *utterly*'

for- is an intensifier, especially in an unpleasant direction: *forbærnan* 'destroy by burning', *forhēawan* 'cut down', *forheard* 'very hard', *forhogian* 'think ill of', *unforcūð* 'not ill-reputed' (4.1.35)

ge- gives a perfective meaning to verbs: *gerǣcan* '*get* by reaching', *gefeohtan* '*get* by fighting', *gefēran* '*reach* by going', *gehlēapan* 'leap *upon*'. This is linked with the notion of *inclusiveness* when used with other parts of speech, as in *gehwǣr* '*every*where'

of- chiefly adds completeness to the meaning of verbs: *ofslēan* 'strike *down*'

tō- is another strong intensifier; *tōberstan* 'break apart, shatter'

Suffixes

-a forms agent nouns from verbs: *sincgifa* 'treasure-giv*er*'

-e forms adverbs from adjectives: *dēope* 'deeply', *fæste* 'firmly', *frēondlīce* 'in a friendly way'

-end forms agent nouns: *gārberend* 'spear-bear*er*'

-lic forms adjectives, especially from nouns: *gōdspellic* 'concerning the gospel, evangelical', *heofonlic* 'heavenly'

-līce forms adverbs from adjectives: *snotorlīce* 'wisely', *witodlīce* 'certainly', *stīðlīce* 'sternly'

-ung forms abstract nouns, especially from verbs: *þrōwung* 'torment', *geendung* 'end'

Glossary

The meanings of words are for the most part explained at the points where they occur in the texts. We give here only a general indication of the meaning (or a grammatical reference) for those items which are not glossed at or near each occurrence. A few words which have remained unchanged in Modern English are omitted. Nouns, pronouns, and verbs are accompanied by grammatical information: for G, see 5.5; AN, 5.6; D, 5.17; N, 5.18.

ac: but
āgan: have (5.20)
āge→āgan
āh, āhte→āgan
āhafen→āhebban
āhebban: raise (N āhefð, āhōf, āhōfon, āhafen)
āhōf, āhōfon→āhebban

æfter: after
ǣlc: each
ǣnig: any
ǣr: before, formerly
ǣrest: first
æt: at, from

bæd, bǣdon→biddan
bær, bǣron→beran
be: by
bearn: child (G n)
behealdan: hold (→healdan)
behēold, behēoldon→behealdan
bēo, bēoð→bēon
bēon: be (5.21)
beorn: man (G m)
beran: bear, carry (N birð, bær, bǣron, geboren)
bīdan: remain (N bītt, bād, bidon, gebiden)
biddan: ask, command (N bitt, bæd, bǣdon, gebeden)
bindan: bind (N bint, band, bundon, gebunden)
bindað, binde, bindeð→bindan
bið→bēon
bond = band→bindan
byrð = birð→beran

cald: cold
cōm, cōme→cuman
const = canst→cunnan
cuman: come (N cym(e)ð, c(w)ōm, c(w)ōmon, gecumen)
cumen = gecumen→cuman
cunnan: know, know how to (5.20)
cunnað→cunnian
cunne, cunnon→cunnan
cunnian: experience (D cunnað, cunnode)
cunnige→cunnian
cūðe, cūðon→cunnan
cwæð→cweðan
cweðan: say, speak (N cwiðð, cwæð, cwǣdon, gecweden)
cwōm, cwōman→cuman
cwyð→cweðan
cymest, cym(e)ð→cuman
cyning: king (G m)

dēah→dugan
dō→dōn
dohte→dugan
dōn: do (dēð, dyde, dydon, gedōn)
dearr: dare (5.20)
dorste→dearr
dōð→dōn
dugan: be of use (5.20)
durre→dearr
dyde, dydon→dōn

ēac: also
eal(l): all
eart→wesan
eft: again
engel: angel (G m)
eom→wesan
ēode, ēodon→gān
eorl: man; but see 3.1, footnote 6 (G m)
eorðe: earth, ground, world (AN f)
ēow, ēower 5.9

faran: go (N færð, fōr, fōron, gefaren)
fareð→faran
fæste: firmly
feaht→feohtan
feala = fela
feallan: fall (N fylð, fēoll, fēollon, gefeallen)
fealleð→feallan
fela: many
feohtan: fight (N fyht, feaht, fuhton, gefohten)
fēol(l), fēollon→feallan
fēond: enemy, devil (G m)
feor: far
feorh: life (G n, gen. sg. fēores)
fēran: go (D fērð, fērde)
fēt→fōt

findan: find (N fint, fand, fundon, gefunden)
flēag→flēogan
flēogan: fly (N flȳð, flēag, flugon, geflogen)
folc: people, band, company (G n)
folde: earth, land (AN f)
folme: hand (AN f)
for: before, because of
forlǣtan: let, leave (→lǣtan)
forlēt, forlēton→forlǣtan
forniman: take (→niman)
fornime→forniman
fornōm, fornōmon→forniman
forð: forth, forward
forðan, forðon: thus
fōt: foot (m 5.7)
fram: from
ful(l): full; very
fundað→fundian
funde, fundon→findan
fundian: set out (D fundað, fundode)
fȳnd→fēond
fȳr: fire (G n)

gā→gān
gān: go (gǣð, ēode, ēodon, gegān)
gangan: go (N gengð, gēng, gēngon, gegangen)
gangon→gangan
gār: spear (G m)
gāð→gān
gǣð→gān
gē 5.9
gebād→gebīdan
gebīdan: wait, experience (→bīdan)
gebiden, gebīdeð→gebīdan
gebindan: hold fast (→bindan)
gebindað→gebindan
gebunden→gebindan
gecunnad→cunnian
gehātan: promise, call (→hātan)
gehāten→hātan
gehealdan: hold, keep (→healdan)
gehealdeð→gehealdan
gehēt→gehātan
gehwylc: each, every
gehȳran: hear (D gehȳrð, gehȳrde)
gehȳrde, gehȳrst→gehȳran
geman→gemunan
gemon = geman→gemunan
gemunan: remember (5.20)
gemunað→gemunan
gemunde, gemundon→gemunan
genāman, genāme, genāmon→geniman
genim→geniman
geniman: take (→niman)
gengde→gengan
gengan: go (D gengeð, gengde)
geond: throughout
georn: eager
georne: eagerly, clearly
gesāwe, gesāwon→gesēon
geseah→gesēon
gesēon: see, perceive (→sēon)
gesēonde→gesēon
gewāt→gewītan
gewinn: battle, struggle (G n)
gewitan: ascertain (→witan)
gewītan: go (N gewītt, gewāt, gewiton, gewiten)
gewītað, gewitene, gewīteð→gewītan
gewyrcan: bring about, earn (→wyrcan)
gewyrce→gewyrcan
geworht→wyrcan
geworhton→gewyrcan
gif: if
gōd: good
gyf = gif

habban: have (D ic hæbbe, hē hæfð, hafað, hæfde)
hafast, hafað→habban
hand: hand (G f)
hātan: command, call (N hǣtt, hēt hēton, gehāten)
hāten = gehāten→hātan
hātte→hātan (5.26)
hæbbað, hæbbe→habban
hæfde, hæfdon, hæfð→habban
hē 5.9
heofon: heaven (G m)
hēoldon→healdan
heora = hira 5.9
heorte: heart (AN f)
hēr: here
hēt, hēton→hātan
hī 5.9
hīe = hī 5.9
hild: battle (G f)
him 5.9
hine 5.9
hira 5.9
his 5.9
hit 5.9
hlāford: lord (G m)
hogode, hogodon→hycgan
hond = hand
hū: how
hwǣr: where
hwæt: what
hwæð(e)re: however
hwīl: while (G f)
hwīlon = hwīlum
hwīlum: sometimes, at times
hȳ = hī 5.9
hycgan: think (D hogað, hogode)
hycge→hycgan
hyge: mind, thoughts (G m)
hym = him 5.9
hyra = hira 5.9
hyse: young man (G m, gen. sg. hys(s)es)
hyt = hit 5.9

ic 5.9
in: in, into

lāgon→licgan
lang: long
læg, lǣge→licgan
lǣtan: let, cause (N lǣtt, lēt, lēton, gelǣten)
leg = læg→licgan
lēof: dear
leofað→libban
lēt, lēton→lǣtan
libban: live (D ic libbe, hē leofað, lifde)
licgan: lie (N līð, læg, lǣgon, gelegen)
licgað, licgende→licgan
līf: life (G n)
lifdon→libban
lifge, lifgende→libban
ligeð→licgan
līð→licgan

magan: be able (5.20)
man: one (5.26)
man(n): man (m 5.7)
maneg = manig
manig: many
mæg, mæge→magan
mænig = manig
mē 5.9
meahte, meahton→magan
mec 5.9
men(n)→man(n)
micel: much, great
mid: with
miht, mihte→magan
mīn 5.9
mōd: spirit, mind (G n)
mon = man
mon(n) = man(n)
monig = manig
mōst, mōste, mōston→mōt
mōt: be able, obliged, allowed (5.20)
mōte, mōton→mōt
mycel = micel

nam→niman
næbbe, næfdon, næfð→habban (5.30)
nǣron→wesan (5.30)
ne, nē 5.29
nim→niman
niman: take (N nimð, nam/nōm, nāmon/nōmon, genumen)
nimað, nime→niman
nis→bēon (5.30)
nō: never
nolde, noldon→willan (5.30)
nū: now

of: from
ofer: over
on: in(to), on(to)
ond: and
ongan→onginnan
ongeat, ongēaton→ongytan
ongietan = ongytan
onginnan: begin (N onginn(e)ð, ongan, ongunnon, ongunnen; 5.24)
onginnað→onginnan
ongunnon→onginnan
ongytan: perceive (N ongytt, ongeat, ongēaton, ongyten)
oð: until
ōðer: other, second
oððe: or

rād→rīdan
rīdan: ride (N rītt, rīdeð, rād, ridon, geriden)
rīdeð→rīdan

saga→secgan
sǣde→secgan
sǣton→sittan
sceal→sculan
sceoldan, sceolde, sceoldon→sculan
sceole, sceolon→sculan
sculan: be obliged to (5.20)
scyle→sculan
se, sē 5.4, 5, 10
sēc, sēce, sēceð→sēcan
sēcan: seek (D sēcð, sōhte)
secgan: say, tell (D ic secge, hē segð, sǣde)
sege→secgan
sende, sendon→sendan
sendan: send (D sent, sende)
sēo 5.4, 5, 10
sēon: see (N syhð, seah, sāwon, gesewen)
sind, sindon→wesan
sittan: sit (N sitt, sæt, sǣton, geseten)
siððan: afterwards
sōhte, sōhton→sēcan
spræc, sprǣcon→sprecan
sprecan: speak (N spric(e)ð, spræc, sprǣcon, gesprecen)
spriceð→sprecan
standan: stand (N stent, stōd, stōdon, gestanden)
standeð→standan
stōd, stōdon→standan
stondað, stondeð = standað, standeð→standan
sum: one, a certain, some
swā: so, as (5.28)
swīðe: very
swurd: sword (G n)
sylf: self
syllan: give (D sylð, sealde)
syllon→syllan
synd, syndon = sind, sindon→bēon

tō: to, as; too

þā: then, when (5.28)
þā 5.4, 5, 10
þām, þāra 5.4, 5, 10
þās 5.4, 6, 10
þǣm 5.4, 5, 10
þǣr: there, where (5.28)

þǣra, þǣre 5.4, 5, 10
þæs 5.4, 5, 10
þæt 5.4, 5, 10
þæt: that (as conjunction)
þe: that, who, which (5.10)
þē 5.9
þēah: though, yet
þencan: think, intend (D þencð, þōhte)
þence, þenceð→þencan
þēoden: prince (G m)
þēos 5.4, 6, 10
þes 5.4, 6, 10
þīn 5.9
þincan: seem (D þincð, þūhte)
þīne, þīnum 5.9
þis 5.4, 6, 10
þone 5.4, 5, 10
þonne: then, when (5.28); than (with comparative)
þū 5.9
þūhte→þincan
þurh: through
þȳs 5.4, 6, 10

ūre 5.9
ūs 5.9

wadan: go, advance (N wædð, wōd, wōdon, gewaden)
wāst→witan
wāt→witan
wǣpen: weapon (G n)
wǣre, wǣron→wesan
wæs→wesan
wē 5.9
wearð→weorðan
weorðan: become (N wyrð, wearð, wurdon, geworden; 5.26)
weorðeð→weorðan
weoruld = woruld
wesan: be (5.21)
wīg: battle (G n)
willan: want (5.20)
wil(l)e, willað→willan
wisse→witan
wiste→witan
witan: know (5.20)
wite→witan
wið: with, towards
wōd, wōdon→wadan
wolde, woldon→willan
word: word (G n)
worhtan, worhte→wyrcan
worold = woruld
woruld: world (G f)
wurdon→weorðan
wylle = wille→willan
wyrcan: make (D wyrcð, worhte)
wyrce, wyrcð→wyrcan

ymb(e): around